T0165274

ACKNOWLEDGEMENT

I sincerely acknowledge and appreciate the contributions of my family, my boss – Mr. Salihu Aliyu Gusau, my mentor – Mr. Sola Owonibi, my friends – Jummai Joseph, Barr. James Ugbeda, Oladejo Olawumi, Mr. Williams Gomez and other numerous contributors towards the success of this publication. May GOD bless you all.

SECOND CHIEF: Well spoken.

KING ABUTU: (*furiously*) what concern has a hyena over the predicament of a lame rabbit that cannot run for safety? Or have you also forgotten that it is the death of the cat that gives room for the rats to make merry in the household of an old woman?!

FIRST CHIEF: Your highness, I absolutely agree with my colleagues. There are villages out there that have been so much intolerant of us as a people that at a mere mention of our names, they spit. Those are our enemies. So why don't we stop warring against our friends and reserve our strength to strategize against our enemies? Aneile is a friendly land currently facing hard times. It is not the right place to search for slaves. Let us look elsewhere my lord.

KING ABUTU: You said Aneile is facing hard times? Have you forgotten that few moons ago Aneile captured over four dozens of Ejule sons as slaves in a fierce battle between the two lands?

SECOND CHIEF: Your highness, Ejule made the same mistake we are about to make now by attacking quiet and peace loving Aneile but somehow, the gods came to their rescue and turned the battle against Ejule.

KING ABUTU: Hear yourself! Are you saying Aneile is harmless and at the same time indomitable?!

SECOND CHIEF: Your highness, what I am saying is that a sluggish old woman that goes about in peace and talks to nobody could cause irrevocable harm if dared unjustly because no one knows what strength she conceals under her tattered wrapper.

KING ABUTU: We are no cowards like Ejule warriors. If the

lion would lose a battle, it cannot be to a dog. Aneile cannot stop us. Warriors!

WARRIORS: Onu jaaaashii!!!

KING ABUTU: (*on his feet*) Rise up and get ready for battle.

WARRIORS: Your highness, we are ready!!! (*Sing war song as they disperse*)

[The chiefs gaze at one another disappointedly as lights fade out and shine on the NARRATOR.]

NARRATOR: *That was how King Abutu refused to heed the counsel of his chiefs and sent his warriors to Aneile. In Aneile on the other hand, the warriors are ready to defend their territory.*

Lights fade out on the Narrator and shine on ANEILE warriors who sing war song as they enter into a kingless palace where the chiefs are already seated and waiting. The attires and adornments of the chiefs and warriors are similar to those of UJAYAN save for white shorts worn by the warriors and deeper costume in terms of colorations and charms. The warriors are led by their commander named Obaje.

OBAJE: (*Squats*) Elders of ANEILE, Ujayan warriors are already at the mouth of our village. We are going there right now to put a stop to their advancement and tell them that though the wasp may have been soaked by the rain, but that does not give the ear the effrontery to sweep its comb.

FIRST ELDER: (*on his feet*) calm down warriors. It is true that the fact that the crocodile's teeth are sore does not give the fowl the audacity to scramble for food in its mouth but it is also true that the hunter who rushes at his game on a slippery ground loses not only the game but also the traces of its footprints as well. Be patient young ones.

SECOND ELDER: And remember, a man who climbs a delicate tree hastily crashes down heavily.

THIRD ELDER: Besides, no barefooted man hurries to get past a thorny jungle.

FOURTH ELDER: And do not forget that it takes caution to chase a viper in dry vegetation.

OBAJE: Elders of Aneile, we thank you all for your wisdom. Today I believe in the saying of our people that where elders are present, the dropping phlegm has no abode in the mouth of an orphan. We shall take caution as you have all advised. May we now go and defend our destiny.

FIRST ELDER: Warriors of Aneile!

WARRIORS: Elders of our land!!!

FIRST ELDER: Are you all battle ready?

WARRIORS: Yes we are!!!

SECOND ELDER: Are these all of you?

OBAJE: No elders. Some of us have already laid ambush at the border to prevent any sudden attack.

THIRD ELDERS: What about the slave warriors from Ejule and Ilemona the slave hunter from Abejukolo?

OBAJE: They are among those laying ambush at the border. In fact, Ilemona is the commander of our right wing troop.

THIRD ELDER: That was a wise decision by you.

[*The rest elders nod in support.*]

OBAJE: Thank you elders.

FOUTH ELDERS: I hope you are all with your weapons?

OBAJE: You elders say that no serpent leaves its venom at home when it goes out hunting. We are armed to the tooth.

FIRST ELDER: Obaje!

OBAJE: Old one, your son listens.

FIRST ELDER: The dry grasses and fallen leaves grumble at length in darkness, no one knows whether the sound we hear is of a game that delights our pots or is of a spirit that endangers our lives.

OBAJE: With the gods behind us, victory is ours.

SECOND ELDER: The hope of the unborn child, the joy of our children, the future of our youth and the salvation of the elders of this land rest on the outcome of this battle. If we win, we shall die no more, but if we fail, we shall never live to fight another day again.

THIRD ELDER: We have known you all to be great warriors with rare strength, courage and determination. We therefore invoke the guidance of the gods of this land to go with you and help you to victory. May you therefore return home with victory songs.

WARRIORS: May the gods grant the prayer.

FOURTH ELDER: May the outcome of this battle become an event to be celebrated by us and our posterities.

ALL: May the gods grant the prayer.

OBAJE: Our elders, with your blessings and the ritual fortification by Ukpahiu the Chief Priest, we are sure of returning home with victory songs. (*Turns and faces his co-warriors*) warriors!

WARRIORS: eeeeooh!!!

OBAJE: It's time for war. Let's go!

[The warriors turn and move out in straight line with Obaje leading and all sing war song as they depart.]

ELDERS: May the gods of our ancestors be with you all.

[Lights fade out on the palace of ANEILE and shine on the battle field. The battle becomes tense. Some warriors of both lands can be seen exchanging swords and arrows while others wrestle with one another. As the deadly battle proceeds, the pendulum begins to swing towards UJAYAN warriors as they gain upper hand over ANEILE warriors. More of ANEILE warriors fall by the swords and arrows of UJAYAN warriors.]

[Lights fade out on the battle field and shine on Obaje, Ilemona and another warrior by name Edime in a less volatile part of the battle field. The trio breathes profusely and exhaustedly.]

OBAJE: (*Calling and holding him back on the shoulder*) Ilemona!

ILEMONA: eeooh Obaje.

OBAJE: I think the battle is lost.

ILEMONA: (*sharply*) No! For the dead ones, it is over but for those of us still living, to quit on a battle field is nothing but cowardice. We must fight to the end. It is only at the end of a battle that you can tell who a hero is.

EDIME: Ilemona, this is not about heroism; it is about survival. Am afraid, most of our warriors have been killed. The few of us left cannot withstand the strength of Ujayan warriors. They will surely overwhelm us.

OBAJE: (*showing strong approval*). That is what I am saying!!

8

ILEMONA: The fact that we are still alive means we can still alter the situation. It is not by our number but our strength and bravery. Let's go right there and do what heroes are known to do. (*Turning to go*).

OBAJE: (*pulling back Ilemona by the shoulder*). Look, Ilemona, as for me it is a foolish dog that jumps into a flame of aggressive fire to save her burning puppy. I have more important things to do with my life. I don't believe in heroism that will bring tears to my family. I am running away.

ILEMONA: (*shocked*) but that is cowardice!

OBAJE: If cowardice would give me hope of seeing another day, then I better be a coward. Of what use is bravery that brings nothing but death to me and grief to my family?!

ILEMONA: (*surprised and shoves him aside*). Ah! Obaje, but you can't do this to your people! You are the commander-in-chief of Aneile warriors. What do you expect those you command to do when you run away from the battle field? After all, you know…. that what the lion sees and runs from, the dog does not wait to see.

OBAJE: Ilemona, mother-hen does not offer herself in exchange of her egg been consumed by the serpent. I have made up my mind. I am leaving!

ILEMONA: What will you tell the elders when you get back to the village?

OBAJE: When fire consumes a fowl, you don't expect the tale of the tragedy to be told by feathers. By the time Ujayan warriors exterminate you all here; they would go right into the village and destroy everybody there. I am not going back to Aneile. I have already sent my wife and our children to her village in *Agojeeju* to take refuge. So what business do I have again in Aneile?

sprinkles the powder freely into the air. Instantaneously, UJAYAN warriors drop dead one after the other until no single sole is left standing. Handfuls of the fallen ANEILE warriors rise up one after the other. Upon realizing that it was Ilemona that saved their lives, they lift him up shoulder high and sing victory songs.

ILEMONA: (*helps himself down*) great warriors of Aneile!

WARRIORS: Yes great warlord!!!

ILEMONA: Let us match straight down to UJAYAN and destroy their heartless king, chiefs and anyone who stands on our way. Warriors are we ready!

WARRIORS: yes great warlord!!!!

[Lights fade out and shine on the NARRATOR.]

NARRATOR: *That was how Ilemona helped ANEILE to a glorious victory over UJAYAN. He saved the land from possible extinction. At UJAYAN on the other hand, everybody including the recalcitrant king Abutu and his chiefs, have being alerted of the danger ahead.*

[Lights fade out and shine on UJAYAN.]

ABUTU: (*bears his two hands on his head*) I am finished!

FIRST CHIEF: (*disappointedly*) we warned you your highness but you wouldn't listen. You have forgotten that the chick that refuses to heed its mother's counsel would end up in the belly of a voracious hawk.

SECOND CHIEF: Anyone who fornicates with disobedience must be prepared to bear the pregnancy of shame and regret. Now that the head of the rat is already in the mouth of the cat, what do we do to save its thighs from been consumed?

THIRD CHIEF: Your highness, the cow that remains adamant

to fight the rock with its horns must be prepared to nurse a broken head. No amount of prayer can deliver a rabbit who slaps the hyena on the face. We are in for destruction!

KING ABUTU: (*looks into the sky*) gods of our ancestors, where were you when our warriors were been consumed like dry grasses attacked by wild fire? We are in trouble!

FIRST CHIEF: (*aggressively*) your highness, just leave the gods out of this! You have forgotten that a man who out of his own volition jumps into a deep pit, the gods do not help him to have a safe landing. We counseled you that docile people are dangerous people but stubbornness wouldn't allow you reason. Now that you have put us into trouble, where do we run to?

KING ABUTU: When a child sees something frightening, he runs away. The day the pigeon losses its wings to catapult is the day it ceases to be bird. Let everyone take his or her belongings and run away to nearby villages before Aneile warriors condemn us into the dustbin of history.

SECOND CHIEF: Are we not already condemned into the dustbin of history? Fellow Chiefs of Ujayan, when the hurricane takes control of a dead forest, he who takes refuge under a delicate tree must run before calamity befalls him. What are we still waiting for when the mighty tree is already cracking? Are we going to remain here to allow the king's obstinacy destroy us?

FIRST AND THIRD CHIEFS: Yes you are right. We have to leave now!!

KING ABUTU: (angrily) listen, you foolish chiefs! The fact that a palm wine tapper crashes down from the top of a palm tree does not make him cease being a man. Was I supposed to follow your directive as your king? Or does the wailing of the young birds prevent their mother from hunting? Don't you *and dance. Lights fade out on the crowd and shine on the NARRATOR.]*

NARRATOR: *That was how ILEMONA the slave hunter from Abejukolo became the King of ANEILE. The people were so happy, healthy, fruitful and prosperous under his reign and a day was also set aside to celebrate the victory of the land over UJAYAN.*

ILEMONA rules for about forty-four years and he has now fallen in love with old age. He barely could walk by now. He has only a child named ONUCHOWGU from his late wife. Knowing that he might soon go the way of his ancestors, he sends for ONUCHOWGU.

[Lights fade out on the NARRATOR and shine on ILEMONA sitting on his throne. The palace is decorated with elephant tusks, buffalo horns, leopard skin and other assorted traditional ornaments.]

ONUCHOWGU: (*pays homage and then squats*) yes father, here I am.

ILEMONA: Onuchowgu my son, I have called you for an important matter.

ONUCHOWGU: What is it, father?

ILEMONA: I have told you my life history and how I emerged as the king of this land.

ONUCHOWGU: Yes father, you have, but what about that?

ILEMONA: You can see by yourself that I am not getting younger anymore. When a fruit ripens on top of a tree, it knows its end is near. I am about ending my journey in life to join my ancestors in the great beyond.

ONUCHOWGU: Father; please don't talk like that. You will not die now.

ILEMONA: My son, I am like a ripe fruit whose link to its ancestral origin is weakened by age and soon to bid farewell to the tree top. As you know, you are my only child and tradition demands that when I die, you will take over the mantle of authority. You must rule with great wisdom just the way you have seen me ruled. The greatest task in life is the task of leadership. You must not give rooms for mistakes as a single mistake you make can cost your kingdom dearly. You must be just and fair to everyone. There must be no sacred cows in this land. Whoever goes against the law must be made to face the wrath of the law. Listen to the wise counsel of your subjects and make most decisions after due consultations with your chiefs and elders of the land. Let the welfare and happiness of your people be your utmost considerations in all your actions and decisions. Be steadfast and courageous. Trials and temptations will come but you must be calm and believe that no matter how forceful and fierce the thunder strikes, it can never frighten the sky that shelters it. Control your temper and adjourn proceedings that tend to throw you in anger. The gods of our ancestors will guide and protect you. I hope you will remember my words in the future my son.

ONUCHOWGU: (*soberly*) yes father, I will. I shall do as you have advised.

ILEMONA: (*stands up*) thank you my son. You may go now. I need to go in and rest. (*Exit Ilemona*)

[*Light fades out on the palace and shines on the NARRATOR.*]

NARRATOR: *Few moons later, King Ilemona joins his ancestor and Onuchowgu takes over as king of ANEILE.*

[*Two men come forward and invest ONUCHOWGU in royal robes and crown while the TOWN'S PEOPLE sing, dance, pay homage and then disperse*]

He followed to the letters the counsel of his father and the land became more fruitful and more prosperous than it was during the reign of his father.

However, strange things begin to happen. Calamity looms in the land. An unprecedented abomination is being hatched in the land. The life and reign of ONUCHOWGU are about to crumble. The land itself is on the verge of extinction as some men begin to wrestle with GOD! There seemed to be no way out.

[TOWN'S PEOPLE sing dirge and suddenly begin to run helter-skelter with no invader in sight]

The questions are: who is at fault? Has the end come for ONUCHOWGU and his generation? Who will win the contest between the men and GOD in Aneile? Will ANEILE survive even when its extinction has become obvious in the horizon?

Hold on tight to your horse and gallop forward to see the present situation in ANEILE and find out the answers to those questions.

[Lights fade out on the NARRATOR.]

ACT ONE SCENE ONE

Lights shine on the king's bedroom. The room is well decorated with animal horns and skins all hanging on the walls. There is a wooden bed neatly made up. There is a pair of stools each placed on the side of the bed with each bearing a small pot. There are charms made of cowries, beads, jewelries and masks of various shapes and sizes signifying the images of the village's deities and masquerades placed on stools and hung on the walls. Queen Ajanigo bends by the corner of the room arranging her jewelries in a box. The king enters, sits on the bed, picks a container of snuff, gives it a knuckle, opens, takes a little quantity and begins to inhale)

AJANIGO: *(notices his presence, walks to him and kneels beside him)* my lord, you don't look happy. What is the matter?

ONUCHOWGU: Nothing my queen.

AJANIGO: *(After a pause)* my lord, a man does not grow goose pimples on his body without a reason. You don't look happy and I know that something bothers you. My lord I am your wife. Please tell me what it is that bothers you.

ONUCHOWGU: Ajanigo my queen, when the rat suddenly discovers the plot of the ratter, it ceases to laugh in the open place. That is the cause of my sorrow.

AJANIGO: My lord, who is plotting what?

ONUCHOWGU: (*after a pause*) Ajanigo my dear wife, the chimpanzee that has known no land other than the land of the gorillas calls the gorillas its brethren but the gorillas say they are not related, who shall accommodate the chimpanzee if the gorillas eventually put their words into action?

AJANIGO: My lord, who are the gorillas and who is the chimpanzee?

ONUCHOWGU: You remember how my father was chosen by the kingmakers in consultation with the gods as the king of Aneile?

AJANIGO: Yes I do my lord.

ONUCHOWGU: The people are saying I am no longer fit for the throne!

AJANIGO: (*shocked*) what! (*After a pause*) were the gods not behind the choice of your father and you as kings?

ONUCHOWGU: Of course my queen.

AJANIGO: And the entire villagers were happy about it; how come that they are rejecting you now?

ONUCHOWGU: They said they are tired of been ruled by slaves!

AJANIGO: They must be out of their senses. By the way my lord, who in particular are the people involved?

ONUCHOWGU: My wife, the betrothed hen has been raped

by unruly cocks in her neighborhood and she has now laid some eggs as a result. The cock to which she is betrothed chooses to find the culprits among the cocks in the neighborhood; but now that the eggs have not yet been hatched, no one can tell which cocks are responsible.

AJANIGO: My lord, you have once said to me that a farmer who makes his farm in the territory of the monkeys need not consult a seer before he knows that his missing banana is the handwork of the monkeys. I suspect your chiefs!

ONUCHOWGU: (*surprised and gazes at her in awe*) you do?

AJANIGO: Yes my lord. We both know that it takes an elephant to bring down an elephant.

ONUCHOWGU: (*helps her sit beside him on the bed*) Ajanigo, my queen, I had a similar thought but I had to fault it on the ground that as chiefs who know the customs and traditions of this land better than anyone else, they will not dare challenge what the gods approved.

AJANIGO: I think my lord is underestimating the capabilities of his chiefs.

ONUCHOWGU: May be.

AJANIGO: (*after a pause*) By the way my lord, who told you about the conspiracy?

ONUCHOWGU: Omale the village old tale bearer told me about it.

AJANIGO: My lord, the words of tail bearers are like the words of drunkards, nobody knows which to believe or disbelieve.

ONUCHOWGU: He keeps on telling me about it day by day and you know when a dog sniffs continuously at a hole, a wise hunter does not overlook it.

AJANIGO: My lord, why didn't he tell you those behind the plot?

ONUCHOWGU: He claims not to know them. The only thing he claimed to know is that there is a plot by some people to dethrone me.

AJANIGO: My lord, what do we do?

ONUCHOWGU: Like I told you earlier, the eggs have not been hatched for us to know which of the cocks in the neighborhood raped the mother-hen. Even though we are both suspecting my chiefs, we have to exhaust all investigative machineries before pointing accusing fingers at anybody otherwise our case will be like the case of a wicked step mother who at the mere mention of a wrongdoing in the house, she unjustly accuses her motherless step child.

AJANIGO: You are right my lord.

ONUCHOWGU: (*lies down*) I am expecting some visitors from Ankpa. They have a message for me from their king. I need to rest before they come.

AJANIGO: That would be necessary my lord. (*She rises up and goes back to her box of jewelries*)

Lights fade out and shine on the palace.

ACT ONE SCENE TWO

The palace of ANEILE maintains the same decoration it has during the reign of Ilemona. Two guards stand behind the throne, a pair by the entrance of the door and one who appears to be the chief guard moves round the palace as routine security ramble all armed with spears and matchets. Omale sits and waits for the king. The Royal Bard leads the way as the king appears.

ROYAL BARD: The great elephant that treads the land to shake the foundations of the earth, the iroko tree that rules the jungle of great trees; the eagle on the hill crest whose exploits in the air are too arduous a task for other birds, *Onu jaaashii!* I greet you your highness.

[Everybody pays homage.]

ONUCHOWGU: (*Looks troubled*) it shall be well with you all. (*Calling*) Aduku!

ADUKU: (*Runs in and pay homage*) onu jaaashii - My lord!

ONUCHOWGU: Take my words to Ebiloma that Ankpa

emissaries are on their way to our land; he should mobilize his colleagues to receive them at the border immediately.

ADUKU: Consider it done my lord.

ONUCHOWGU: Go now! (*Exit Aduku; Onuchowgu sits*) Omale, the voice of the night echoes in the jungle, what we do not know is whether the voice we hear is the making of the melodious nightingale or that of the horrendous night owl. Friends or foes, which one have you figured out behind the dark night?

OMALE: Friends but as foes your majesty.

ONUCHOWGU: You mean my acquaintances?

OMALE: Yes my lord!

ONUCHOWGU: Could you please unmask them.

OMALE: My lord; some of the people with whom you make your decisions are involved!

ONUCHOWGU: All of them?

OMALE: That I cannot say for now my lord. We shall be more vigilant to be able to see what the night is hiding.

ONUCHOWGU: Thank you Omale, you may go now. I will send for you as soon as the need arises. However, if there is anything urgent that you think I should know of, don't hesitate to let me know. Is that understood?

OMALE: Yes my lord. Your wish is always my command my lord. (*Pays homage; exit*)

ACT ONE SCENE THREE

Same place; moments later.

(Enter Anibe and pays homage)

ONUCHOWGU: Anibe, what can I do for you?

ANIBE: My lord, you elders say that a child does not see an enemy setting a trap for its father and keeps it a secret. I found out something very shocking that I cannot hide from you my lord because even though I am supposed to be an errand boy in this palace, you have always treated me like your own son. I am an orphan but I have never missed my parent because you have always been there for me.

ONUCHOWGU: (*curiously*) Anibe spare me this sermon! What is it that you want?

ANIBE: My lord, it is about Elder Omale, the village old tale bearer that just left here now.

ONUCHOWGU: And what about him?

ANIBE: My lord, Arome my closest friend confided in me that your chiefs together with Elder Omale held a meeting in his master's house few days ago and he was asked by his master - Chief Ebiloma - to get them some cola nuts. According to him, as he was about to enter and deliver the cola nuts, he heard something that shocked him and decided to retreat at first before eventually going in.

ONUCHOWGU: (*curiously*) what was it that he heard?

ANIBE: That the chiefs and Elder Omale were discussing how to overthrow you!

ONUCHOWGU: (shocked) do you mean what you just said?

ANIBE: Yes my lord. I doubted him when he first told me until the day you sent me to call you Elder Omale. I met the chiefs in his house.

ONUCHOWGU: And you are sure you are telling me the truth?

ANIBE: Yes my lord. I know the consequences of lying to a king especially when it has to do with a sensitive matter as this.

ONUCHOWGU: The abandoned palm tree that fills the gourd of the wine tapper when he prepares for a festival wins the love of the wine tapper and a dog that brings home its game deserves to be rewarded with fleshy bones. I have just discovered how much you love your king. Henceforth, you cease to be a servant in this palace and instead I recognize you as a member of my family.

ANIBE: (awed). My lord, I, a member of a royal family?!

ONUCHOWGU: You have just heard me right.

ANIBE: (hysterical and prostrates) my lord, I am short of

words. I lack words to thank you enough. May your days be long on the throne of your father.

ONUCHOWGU: Now listen. Henceforth you will be working hand in hand with Okpanachi my son. Both of you shall go around the village and mount surveillance on the Chiefs and Omale. You shall both confidentially gather information about their activities back to me.

ANIBE: (*still prostrating*) consider it done my lord. May the gods of our ancestors bring your foes under your feet.

[*Exit Anibe; under the gaze of absent-minded Onuchowgu. Lights fade out*]

ACT ONE SCENE FOUR

Chiefs of Aneile meet in an open thatched house. Two bamboo-made benches are placed opposite each other. A resting wooden chair divides the benches in the north and a stool in the south. Abalaka and Ocheja sit on the right, Idachaba sits alone on the left while the wooden chair and stool remain unoccupied.

ABALAKA: (*clears his throat*) Chiefs of Aneile you are welcome once again.

IDACHABA & OCHEJA: Thank you.

ABALAKA: Chiefs, we have violated the rule of punctuality today. I know that the toad does not hesitate to where the winged termites celebrate unless its limb hurts. What happened to us? Even Chief Ebiloma is not here yet.

OCHEJA: Ufedo my daughter was indisposed. I went to Agudoko forest to collect herbs for her mother.

ABALAKA: I hope her health is improving now.

OCHEJA: Thank be to the gods.

IDACHABA: My friend who came to visit me from Okpo left this afternoon and I had to see him off across the border. And you know when two old friends meet it is always like two long lost lovers reuniting. They always find it hard to part ways again.

(Abalaka and Ocheja concur coinciding with the entrance of Ebiloma.)

EBILOMA: *(sits on the wooden chair)*. My fellow chiefs I am sorry for coming late. My cousin came from Idah to inform me about his upcoming marriage taking place in Ayangba. I am the one standing as his father.

CHIEFS: That is alright.

EBILOMA: Thank you elders. Now what is today's agenda?

ABALAKA: We are still ruminating on how to seek and obtain the support of Ogecha the Chief Priest.

EBILOMA: So what do we do?

OCHEJA: We are no longer kids. We all know that to uproot a tree, one must get rid of the roots that hold it to the ground. Let us set our eyes on the gods!

(Chiefs gaze at one another in surprise)

ABALAKA: Chief Ocheja, no matter how drunk the maggot may be, it does not stagger to the territory of the shoulder ants and challenge them to a battle. Or has the rock become so soft that the cricket now dreams of burrowing a mansion in it? How can mortals fight immortals?

CHIEFS: *(with the exclusion of Ocheja)* it is impossible!!!

IDACHABA: The imbecility of an antelope cannot drive it to challenge the lion to a wrestling contest. The cockroach that goes to trouble the hen in her house digs its own grave. Daring the gods is daring destruction!

EBILOMA: Chief Ocheja, you see, (*pointing*) Chief Abalaka and Chief Idachaba have said it all. A well dressed butterfly that chooses to put out a burning fire shall be stripped naked. Let us not lay down our palms to bear hot embers so that we don't subject our alms to unbearable pains. There is no way we can succeed in getting rid of the gods. What we only need is the support of Ogecha the Chief Priest.

OCHEJA: How do we get Ogecha to support us?

EBILOMA: (*after a pause*) I think I have a solution to that.

CHIEFS: (*curiously*) what is the solution?

EBILOMA: When the teeth suffer severe ache, the tongue seizes the opportunity to control the meat.

CHIEFS: What does that mean?

EBILOMA: Chiefs, remember that the King and the Chief Priest are no longer in good terms.

CHIEFS: (*anxiously*) yes.

EBILOMA: Let's capitalize on that and draw the Chief Priest to our side.

IDACHABA: That makes a lot of sense. A man who befriends the bee taps the honey with ease.

OCHEJA: Chiefs of Aneile, remember that the lioness would not deliver her cub to a hungry hyena simply because the cub is crippled. The sour relationship between the King and the Chief Priest may not be enough reason for the Chief Priest to work against him.

ABALAKA: I agree with Chief Ocheja. Distance is no hindrance to the protection of the cobra over her eggs. It doesn't look easy as it sounds. Ogecha, we all know, has served the gods and the king for many decades and thinking of making him withdraw his loyalty to them is like making a left-handed man right-handed at his old age.

CHIEFS: It is a very difficult task.

EBILOMA: Well, difficult as it may, we have to try first. Who knows, fortune may smile at the young wolf and it meets a dying buffalo on the day its hunting has failed to produce a game.

IDACHABA: I agree with you. But who do we send?

OCHEJA: That would not be a problem. Any of us could go after all.

[Enter Omale]

OMALE: Chiefs of Aneile, I greet you all.

CHIEFS: We greet you too Elder Omale.

(Omale sits on the stool directly facing Ebiloma)

OCHEJA: Is there anything we should know from the palace?

OMALE: There is nothing for now. He is beginning to be consumed by too much anxiety. So it is better to give him some breathing space otherwise he could explode and tear me apart the way a starving lion tears apart the thighs of an antelope.

(All laugh mockingly)

EBILOMA: The last time I was at the palace, the King sounded intimidating with the way he spoke to me.

OCHEJA: The thunder can only grumble, it cannot bring down the sky to the ground. There is nothing he can do to us.

ABALAKA: My fellow chiefs, subject to your approval, may I nominate Elder Omale to meet with the chief priest. Perhaps he would know the best way to convince him.

CHIEFS: That is a good idea.

IDACHABA: Elder Omale, will you be able to do this?

OMALE: Do you ask a rotten meat whether it can smell? (*Chiefs laugh*) and what do you want me to tell the chief priest?

IDACHABA: To seek and obtain the support and cooperation of the Chief Priest.

OCHEJA: Chief Ebiloma would give you the details after this meeting.

ABALAKA: What else do we discuss again?

EBILOMA: Chiefs of Aneile, the night owl hoots only when the night takes charge of the land. We have nothing to discuss until we seek and obtain the cooperation and support of the Chief Priest. We shall converge again as soon as Elder Omale returns from the Chief Priest's house.

[Exeunt chiefs; after exchanging greetings.]

ACT ONE SCENE FIVE

Onuchowgu on casual wears relaxes in the inner chambers of the palace. He sits on a traditional resting wooden chair and absent-mindedly fondles with his royal scepter.

[Enter Okpanachi and Anibe and pay homage.]

ONUCHOWGU: (*sits upright*) my sons, what have you for the king?

OKPANACHI: Father; Arome the servant of Chief Ebiloma hinted Anibe that the chiefs together with Elder Omale would be holding a meeting at an undisclosed venue earlier today. So, the moment Elder Omale left the palace, we decided to trail him, knowing fully he was going to be part of the meeting.

ONUCHOWGU: (*curiously*) was he?

OKPANACHI: Yes, father; but unknown to us, the meeting was almost concluded when he got there. We couldn't get close to get a full gist of what actually transpired as at the time we got there for fear of been found out. But one thing we clearly heard was the task given to Elder Omale.

ACT TWO SCENE ONE

At the palace. Ogecha waits. Enter Onuchowgu. Ogecha and the guards pay homage. He sits.

OGECHA: Your highness, I have come to honour your call.

ONUCHOWGU: Mouthpiece of the gods, you are welcome. How are the gods?

OGECHA: Always fine my lord.

ONUCHOWGU: Do they have any message for me?

OGECHA: Your highness, food that is meant for the stomach is never kept in the mouth. There is no message for now my lord.

ONUCHOWGU: Mother-hen speaks to her chicks at all time to warn of impending dangers; it speaks when there is a hawk close by in the air and also speaks when the hawk is afar; but now, she no longer speaks; not even when hawks are swiftly threatening to prey on her fattest chick. This has never happened in Aneile. I hope there is no abomination in the

Land that has warranted this long silence and I also hope that the message is not being kept from me for any reason.

OGECHA: Your highness, the excreta of a man who suffers from a running stomach is asking to be urgently freed; if the man refuses to let it go out, one of these two would happen to him: he is either disgraced with a stinking soiled pant or he faces an unbearable excruciating bellyache. My case as the mouthpiece of the gods is not different my lord. The gods do not spare anyone who holds back their messages. Besides, they have not complained of any abomination in the Land.

ONUCHOWGU: Ogecha, the mouthpiece of the gods, in whatever you do, the gods and your conscience should always be placed first. Do not allow any personal interest interfere with your sacred duties.

OGECHA: I hope my lord is not distrusting me?

ONUCHOWGU: When an elder winks his eye to a child found on the wrong side of the public, it is not a reproach but a polite way to counsel and caution the child. I have nothing against you but beware, the world is slippery; we must tread it with caution.

OGECHA: Thank you my lord. But I know that something worries my king because the emotion of a man is discernible from his words. What is it that bothers you my lord?

ONUCHOWGU: I had a nightmare!

OGECHA: (*curiously*) nightmare?

ONUCHOWGU: Yes nightmare.

OGECHA: What did you see my lord?

ONUCHOWGU: I saw a priest who was a custodian of a village Oracle. The land had been severely terrorized by evil forces. To put a stop to this, the gods presented the priest with an axe and instructed him to cut down certain evil trees in the land. Sometime later, four witches visited the priest to persuade him to release the sacred axe to them. He let go the axe after succumbing to the offers of large amount of cowries and treasures the witches offered him. The witches went back to their groove and neutralized the power of the axe thereby rendering it impotent. Calamity doubled in the land and people hitherto dying in tens started dying in hundreds. I saw myself as a prominent son of the land. I was so terrified that I woke up sweating. What sort of omen could that be?

OGECHA: (*after a pause*) my lord, I understand it to be an omen of impending doom that awaits one of the neighboring villages which you hold so dear. It cannot happen to Aneile because the gods of our ancestors have sworn to be personally involved at all time in protecting this land. They have promised that no evil will ever befall this land. And you know the gods are not like we mortals that make and don't keep promises.

ONUCHOWGU: Ogecha beware!

OGECHA: (*amazed*) of what my lord?

ONUCHOWGU: Beware of the fact that he who allows the deliciousness of a roasted meat fans the embers of dispute between his teeth and his tongue destroys the comfort of the tongue and loses the pleasures and appetite for mastication!

OGECHA: My lord, are you in any way suspecting any unrighteous act on my part against anyone in the land?

ONUCHOWGU: I have not said so.

OGECHA: (*troubled*) my lord; when an inferno consumes the roof of a house, the bricks become uncomfortable. With due respect my lord; your words are not too pleasant today. I pray you my lord, if there is anything you know or that you have heard about me against you or against anyone that I have done or proposes to do advertently or inadvertently, please let me know so that I can make amend.

ONUCHOWGU: Ogecha, the mouthpiece of the gods, venomous flies now fly around; my gourd is in your care; do not open it lest they poison my wine. Our sacred chicks have gone to roost in your neighborhood; I can smell some evil shrews around them; hold tight your rod and don't let them penetrate lest misfortune rules the land. I have a feeling that the priest I saw in my nightmare will be reborn in Aneile. We have to prevent it by all means possible.

OGECHA: My lord, put your mind at rest. The gods are in control.

ONUCHOWGU: (*gesticulates affirmatively*) yes I know and I hope they will not be hindered.

OGECHA: No one hinders the gods my lord.

ONUCHOWGU: We are at the end of the farming season. I hope all the preparatory rituals for the second *Egu Orumamu festival* have been performed.

OGECHA: (*sets to leave*) yes my lord. What ought to be done as at now have been done. We are only waiting for the big day itself. May we witness it my lord.

ONUCHOWGU: May it please the gods

OGECHA: Good bye for now my lord. (*Pays homage, exit*)

Onuchowgu gazes absent-mindedly towards the direction taken by Ogecha. Lights fade out.

ACT TWO SCENE TWO

Omale comes out of his room with a gourd of palm wine. He sits on a log of wood lying adjacent to another log of equal size.

OMALE: Ocholi! (*No response*) Ocholi!! (*No response*) Ocholi!!!

OCHOLI: (*runs out*) naaam baba!

OMALE: Are your ears on holiday?!

OCHOLI: No baba.

OMALE: Were you in coma?

OCHOLI: No baba.

OMALE: Then why did it take a gunshot to awaken your ears?

OCHOLI: I am sorry baba. I was at the stable feeding the animals.

OMALE: And you also fed them with your ears! Go to your

mother's room and get me a wine cup. I wonder why she didn't bring those cups back to my room.

(*Exit Ocholi; enter Chief Ebiloma*)

EBILOMA: *The eye of the eagle* I greet you.

OMALE: *The wisdom of old*, I greet you too.

(*Ebiloma sits on the adjacent log; enter Ocholi; greets Ebiloma and drops a calabash cup*) go back and bring another cup.

EBILOMA: For me?

OMALE: Yes, for you.

EBILOMA: Elder Omale; no matter how serious the hunger may be, a toad running past the viper's territory does not wait to catch insect; safety first before food. What is the outcome of your visit to the Chief Priest?

OMALE: Is that why you will not have a drink?

EBILOMA: Elder Omale; that is an agendum for another day.

OMALE: Ocholi, you may go. (*Exit Ocholi*) Chief Ebiloma; you shouldn't have bordered coming. The water sent down from the sky must end its journey on the land. You know I must definitely come to you to deliver the outcome of the message to you.

EBILOMA: We know you will come. But you see, a child whose father promises a cricket from the farm is always eager to see the father's arrival. It is such eagerness that has driven me here now. The sweet melody of the nightingale or the terrifying hooting of the owl, which one has the night brought for us?

OMALE: The hyena yells loudly; it sounds like both cry and

41

ACT TWO SCENE THREE

The Chief Priest sits on a stool in his room adorned with cowries, shells, horns, animal skulls and skin, masks and carved images of deities. He lifts his pot of herbs and serves himself in a calabash. As he gulps down the herbs, the chiefs enter with greetings. They make themselves comfortable as the Chief Priest is still busy drinking his herb.

CHIEFS: The mouthpiece of the gods we greet you once again.

OGECHA: (*putting down the calabash*) Chiefs of Aneile, I greet you all.

CHIEFS: We hope all is well, wise one.

OGECHA: Waist pain troubles me a lot this day.

EBILOMA: We can't blame the body. It's a response to a long years of hard labour not nurtured with adequate rest.

(*The rest chiefs gesticulate in support*)

OGECHA: That's true.

EBILOMA: Wise one, we have come to honour your call.

OGECHA: You are all welcome.

CHIEFS: Thank you wise one.

OGECHA: Chiefs of Aneile, did the parrot misinterpret the message it was sent or was the message well communicated as sent?

EBILOMA: If we may know wise one, what exactly did the parrot say?

OGECHA: That you are plotting to dethrone King Onuchowgu and you want me to be part of it!

EBILOMA: If those were the words of the parrot, the message was well communicated as sent wise one?

OGECHA: (*harshly*) what gave the dog the impetus to solicit for the alliance of the hyena to dethrone the lion? Is the dog not digging its own grave?

EBILOMA: wise one, We……..

OGECHA: (*cuts in furiously*) listen! A man's heart is so unfair to him that it makes him desire at times even what his creator cannot afford for himself; such a desire kills faster than the venom of a demonic viper. Can the tree be so drunk as to want to bear the land on which it grows on its own head? Why would an ordinary shrimp with just a tilapia as its godfather dreams of spitting on the face of a shark? Has our king become a man's apparel that he can dispose of at his pleasure?

EBILOMA: Wise one, when an easy going dog suddenly barks continuously without stopping; let its spectators not accuse it of been a nuisance; a bad omen may be at a close distance

Could you please tell us how Ilemona, Onuchowgu's father emerged as the King of Aneile.

OGECHA: You mean I should tell you a story that is known even to an unborn child?

IDACHABA: Wise one, it is not lack of skill that makes the monkey ask the squirrel some secrets of the tree top but the need to prevent avoidable mistakes on delicate branches on which the squirrel specializes. We only seek better understanding wise one.

OGECHA: It is no news that it was Ilemona, Onuchowgu's father that saved Aneile from the hands of Ujayan warriors. The gods, *ibegwu* our ancestors, the king makers and the people of Aneile chose him as King of Aneile in appreciation for his heroism.

OCHEJA: Wise one, assuming without conceding that it was Ilemona that saved Aneile from the hands of Ujayan warriors, does the fact that the weeds have helped the farmer to prevent erosion on his farmland give such weeds a licence to outgrow the crops and take possession of the farm? There are many ways to compensate one's personal deity for its favour and blessings one of which is not to behead one's own self for the deity's consumption. We have gone too far in appreciating the bravery of Ilemona by making him king. Now a dynasty of ruling slaves has been unwisely created with Onuchowgu succeeding his father!

OGECHA: (*provoked*) then go and dethrone him and take over. If the hyenas are tired of the dominion of the lions; the solution is simple; they should go to the den and exterminate the lions and then crown themselves as kings of the beasts; of what use is the noise they make about opposing the authority of the lions as kings of the jungle?! Chiefs of Aneile, you are daring the gods of this land; you are daring *ibegwu* our ancestors; you are daring the people of Aneile and you are daring me; the consequences are unbearable; be warned!

(*Chiefs put their heads together for the third time and murmur some conversation*)

EBILOMA: Wise one, we have come to let you know some hidden truth.

OGECHA: (*showing no interest*) what hidden truth?

EBILOMA: Wise one, our respective fathers fought the battle against Ujayan. Edime my father who was the commander of the left wing troop of Aneile warriors told me that your elder brother Obaje the then commander-in-chief of Aneile warriors single-handedly dismantled and annihilated Ujayan army. But due to the fact that your brother together with our own fathers proceeded from the battle field to *Agojeeju* to bring his family back to Aneile, Ilemona was the only leader on ground to lead the victorious warriors back home. Upon arrival, he claimed to be responsible for the victory. That was why the gods, *ibegwu* our ancestors, the Kingmakers and the people were all blinded to choose him as king. The whole arrangement was made easier considering the fact that Ukpahiu the then Chief Priest had a soft spot for Ilemona.

OGECHA: (*sarcastically*) great historian of our time! I can see that you know so much about the past that you can tell the gods their respective dates of birth. You can even tell when *Ojo,* the Supreme Deity came to being. Could you please tell me how my late father met my late mother?

(*Chiefs put their heads together for the fourth time and murmur some conversation*)

EBILOMA: Wise one, if we may ask, has the gods ever complained about anything since Onuchowgu was crowned?

OGECHA: No; the morning sun is cool, friendly and nourishing; that is why the land has nothing to complain about. The gods don't complain for the sake of it unless there is a need to.

ABALAKA: Wise one, no matter how severe is the insanity of the thunder; it does not strike the sky that gives it live.

OGECHA: How do you mean?

OCHEJA: Wise one, reliable information reaching us, revealed that our original gods were lost to the *Jukun* people during their invasion into the whole of *lgala Empire.* Ukpahiu the then Chief Priest with the help of some dubious chiefs imported foreign gods from *Nupe, Idoma, Igbo and Yoruba lands.* Those gods were given the names of our lost gods. Their modes of operations were not understood. Hence, they were easily manipulated and controlled by Ukpahiu through abominable sacrifices. That was why the choice of Ilemona was influenced and they found nothing wrong throughout his reign and now that you are in charge with Onuchowgu the son of Ilemona as king, the gods have not found and will surely never find anything wrong with his administration.

OGECHA: To start with, you as a member of his cabinet and a son of Aneile, what have you found wrong with his administration?

OCHEJA: Wise one, slave ruling free men is what is actually wrong with his administration and that does not portend a good omen for *Aneile.*

CHIEFS: (*gesticulates in consonance*) that is true wise one.

OGECHA: Where were your free men when Aneile was about to be put out of existence by Ujayan? A slave came to your rescue! The dog scares away enemies; that is why it rules the kingdom of domestic animals; the goat, the sheep and the hen have no right to complain since they cannot stand the sight of intruders of their territory. If our free fathers and brothers wanted to be king; they should have made themselves worthy of it. Ascending the throne has never been an act of charity; it is purely on merit where hereditary ascension is disrupted. Our fathers and brothers were not worthy of it. Whom the cap fits has worn it.

(*Chiefs put their heads together for the fifth time and murmur some conversation*)

EBILOMA: Wise one, we believe the imported gods were invoked to enchant the entire villagers so that nobody would be bold enough to come out to say the truth.

OGECHA: Your words tell so much of your level of ignorance. Have you seen where mortals manipulate the immortals? You talk about the gods as if you are referring to your kids at home. Assuming anyone would even want to risk believing you, have you forgotten that we have the *Abifa* the Priest of the Ifa Oracle in *Ayangba* and *Atebo* the Chief Priest of the Royal Ancestral Shrine in *Idah* that spiritually oversee the entire Igala Empire and would have intervened if such abomination was committed in any part of the empire?

CHIEFS: We know.

OGECHA: Good! Then why did they not complain?

OCHEJA: Wise one, if the terrifying venom on the tail of the black scorpion is removed, it fat claws become decorative ornaments enough to frighten only a child and not a man who knows of its impotency. The Ifa Oracle and the Royal Ancestral Shrine cannot function through fictitious gods!

OGECHA: What insanity! I can see that you have all lost your minds.

EBILOMA: Wise one, the cow has been offered daily fresh pastures in a desert; let it choose to eat and leave or reject the meal and starve. We shall give you some time to think about it.

OGECHA: Chiefs of Aneile; does a man need to meditate over an offer to help set his own house on fire when he has an option to say an instant NO? I owe the gods, *ibegwu* my ancestors and the people of Aneile absolute loyalty and under no circumstances shall I allow my personal interest interfere with such loyalty. Hunger cannot drive a sane antelope to graze the pastures grown by the lion. A man of my caliber cannot afford to compromise with his sacred duties for any reason whatsoever. Besides, if you sell combs in the land of the vultures and tortoises, you don't need to be told that you are trading your goods in the wrong market and you are bound to return home without a sale. I am a wrong market for sales of corruption and iniquities; no one trades such goods in me and smiles home with profit. That means I am a bad market for bad products and bad traders like you. Depart you sons of iniquities and don't corrupt me with your abominable talks!

(*Chiefs stand up one after the other*)

EBILOMA: Wise one, he that has chosen an egg for a horse, must be prepared to ride with all extraordinary caution it deserves. We know that as the custodian of the ancestral shrines, it would not be easy for you to accept our proposal just like that. We understand all that and we shall give you time to think about it.

OGECHA: (*furiously*) I say depart you evil men!

(*Elders fidget out one after the other with heads down. Light fades out*)

ACT TWO SCENE FOUR

It is morning; Omale sharpens his cutlass on a stone outside his house. Abalaka enters.

ABALAKA: *Eye of the eagle,* I greet you.

OMALE: Abalaka, I greet you too. *Abu wele kpao odudu?*

ABALAKA: *Lafia.* I can see you are getting set for the farm.

OMALE: (*jokingly*) that is the only way we can have more food in our markets at affordable prices.

ABALAKA: (*smiles*) most importantly our stomachs get their own shares first before our markets.

OMALE: Abalaka, I hope you have come in peace.

ABALAKA: If I have not, I would have drawn my sword by now.

(*Both laugh gently*)

OMALE: I know a river does not overflow its bank if nothing is pressing hard on its weight. What is it Chief of Aneile?

ABALAKA: I have a message for you from the Council of Chiefs.

OMALE: Good or bad?

ABALAKA: The morning sun does not spread bad omen. It is good.

OMALE: Then let me hear it.

ABALAKA: The Chiefs want you to stop visiting the King.

OMALE: (*unhappy*) why?! That I am a basket that cannot hold water?

ABALAKA: Far from it. Following our last meeting, we arrived at so many conclusions and decisions one of which is that all of us should stop visiting the king. We have also constituted a council of kingmakers that shall be responsible for the selection and enthronement of kings in Aneile. We have decided to make you the head of that council which means you are now the *Achadu* of Aneile.

OMALE: (*enthusiastically*) Abalaka are you teasing me or you are serious?

ABALAKA: Elder Omale; that game is for children.

OMALE: (*excitedly*) I am so proud of you chiefs. Now I know I would not regret following you.

ABALAKA: You cannot regret following us. A dog in the company of lions has no regret.

OMALE: I am happy to hear that. By the way, why did you people decide to stop me from visiting the king?

ABALAKA: With the response we got from the Chief Priest on our last visit to him, it seemed the King had succeeded in talking him to his side. That must have been made possible by sufficient information at his disposal about the plot.

OMALE: So you no longer trust me?

ABALAKA: Far from that Elder Omale. What we are saying is that the sky that truly wants to make the land barren does not let its rain visit the earth. The restriction affects us as well.

OMALE: Chief of Aneile, can the particles on the land resist the call of the winds? Do you expect me to turn down the call of the king knowing that such an act is a taboo under our customs and traditions?

ABALAKA: If the king calls you, heed the call but bear it at the back of your mind that a cockroach that frequents the house of an ailing hen to nurse her, may ignorantly be sharpening the hen's beak for its own flesh.

OMALE: (*contentedly*) well, that is not a problem. I wouldn't go to see him unless he sends for me and even if he does, I shall speak no more to him.

ABALAKA: I am delighted to hear that.

OMALE: By the way, has the Chief Priest agreed?

ABALAKA: To consume a bony fish, one must exercise caution. We are still applying all the tactics at our disposal to get his support. Even if he fails us, we have told ourselves that the market is never deserted simply because a popular seller is absent. We are no cowards and we don't fight unfinished battles. (*Sets to go*)

OMALE: I am glad to hear that. Do extend my regards to your fellow Chiefs and tell them that their generosity has made *the eye of the eagle* the happiest man in Aneile today.

ABALAKA: Be sure I will deliver your message. (*Exit*)

OMALE: (*solus*) Hei! Me! A kingmaker! If I am to choose a king, I know what to do. I would order him to come and kneel before me. If he frowns, I would slap him several times until he is no longer fit to be king; and I would choose another person. If that person frowns also, I would bite his nose, his mouth and his ears until he becomes deaf and dumb and no longer fit as king. If my third choice frowns, I would castrate him and he will become fat like an over bloated cow and no longer fit as king. I would drive everybody away and make myself king. Yes! I cannot continue to make kings and not become one. Kingmaker - the king - sounds better! (*Laughs hysterically*)

(*Lights fade out*)

ACT THREE SCENE ONE

Enemaku sharpens his cutlass on a flat stone beside a grinding stone on which Ejura his wife grinds pepper and tomatoes. There are sitting logs placed opposite each other and adjacent to the positioning of Enemaku and Ejura. As he sharpens the cutlass, he pauses occasionally to examine his effort.

EJURA: Baba Omachonu, have you not heard the rumour in town?

ENEMAKU: Oh, about the likely poor yam harvest next year?

EJURA: Ah ah, Baba Omachonu, don't tell me you don't know what is going on in town.

ENEMAKU: Ejura, it is only an idle mind that hunts for rumour. You know I have no time for such.

EJURA: (*Angered*) so it is rumour enh? That your friend King Onuchowgu is about to be thrown out of Aneile is a rumour enh? Okay I am sorry.

ACT THREE SCENE TWO

Onuchowgu sits on his throne, stands, walks up and down the palace looking disturbed. He sits again. Enter Enemaku and pay homage.

ONUCHOWGU: Enemaku, my only true friend, why have you forsaken me the way a fly forsakes a dried up faeces. Am I no longer worthy of your company simply because my body is sore?

ENEMAKU: My lord, no matter how ugly a man's head may be, the neck does not leave it behind when the man pays a visit to the home of a good looking fellow. Our friendship is firmly rooted in sincerity and love.

ONUCHOWGU: Then what made your common bead become a rare commodity in the jewel market?

ENEMAKU: I have been battling with fever for the past three moons and it has kept me indoors for those periods. Even my farms have been overgrown by weeds.

ONUCHOWGU: Accept my apology. I should have sent to know how you are faring but Enemaku my friend; a cock being chased by the crocodile does not wait to crow until it has run to a safe spot. Aggressive shoulder ants have invaded my scrotum; the bites are painful yet I cannot make a kill lest I hurt myself. Now I know no peace.

ENEMAKU: My lord what is it that I hear?

ONUCHOWGU: Enemaku my friend, the earth has turned topsy-turvy that the foundations of our houses have replaced our roofs and our roofs have planted themselves on the ground; we are now sleeping with our heads upside down; how long can we remain in that position?!

ENEMAKU: An abomination?

ONUCHOWGU: Yes, an abomination in Aneile.

ENEMAKU: My lord, what is really going on?

ONUCHOWGU: I am afraid the end of my reign is near.

ENEMAKU: How my lord?

ONUCHOWGU: My chiefs are plotting to dethrone me!

ENEMAKU: So it is true (*curious*) what are you doing about it my lord?

ONUCHOWGU: Enemaku, what can a thatched house do when its owner has made up his mind to set it on fire?

ENEMAKU: My lord, a lion does not doubt his victory when he faces a hyena in battle.

ONUCHOWGU: The case would be different if the hyenas are in battalions against a single lion!

ENEMAKU: My lord, how about seeking the help of your

ACT THREE SCENE THREE

Ogecha sits alone in front his house and meditates.

OGECHA: (*solus*) no, no, what would I tell the gods? That I betray their trust? No, that would be sacrilege otherwise no head rejects the crown. Even an idiot would wish to be king. (*After a pause*) wait, what is this that the King has done?!

There is a FLASH BACK to the event that transpired sometimes back between the King, Enemaku and himself in the palace.

OGECHA: *Your highness, the land in question belongs to my extended family. It was handed down to us by our forefather. After the demise of the Ogijo Anuku – the Head of the extended family, as the next most senior elder, I took over the title and it is expected of me to continue to protect and preserve the land more so that the family shrine is built on it. There is no way anyone can claim what belongs to me and my families not even you Enemaku. (Points at him)*

ENEMAKU: *My lord, the land in question belonged to my grandfather. It was a family land handed down to us by our ancestor from time immemorial. What happened was that my grandfather borrowed some cowries from Elder Ogecha's grandfather and used* the land as collateral with an agreement that upon repayment, the land would be reclaimed. As I was told, my grandfather died the same day he paid back the loan making it impossible to formally reclaim the land. Ever since then till date Elder Ogecha's family has refused to hand over the land to us but instead they gave us some portion of the land to use in the interim. Now they have come to chase us out of that portion on the ground that they want to be in absolute control of their inheritance.

OGECHA: Nothing but a fabricated story!

ONUCHOWGU: Well I have heard both sides. You have given the details as far as you both know. One thing that is not hidden to any elder in Aneile was the tragic death of Enemaku's grandfather and the story is also being told the way Enemaku just told us. Nevertheless, I cannot pronounce any judgment yet. But in the interim, Ogecha, it is my order that you allow Enemaku's family to still hold on to that portion of land given to them pending further deliberations with my cabinet. Soon, we shall invite the both of you with your respective witnesses to come and testify before we conclusively determine the matter.

OGECHA: (disappointed) but your high…..

ONUCHOWGU: Ogecha I have spoken!

(Light fades out and shines back on Ogecha) Me? To lose the land on which I commune with my family ancestral spirit to Enemaku? No way; I can't allow that to happen. How do I explain to posterity that it was under my reign as the head of the family that we lost our family inheritance to some trespassers?

Simply because Onuchowgu is Enemaku's friend he judged partially. This is a bad omen. If a baby cobra is already terrorizing its neighbourhood at a tender age, what magnitude

ONUCHOWGU: Ajanigo; itching of a wound is a harbinger of recovery but if it is an itching ailment, what signs does it give to tell of its intended departure?

AJANIGO: It is actually confusing my lord. We have not seen a sign of an end to this trouble more so that the gods are not talking. What do you think would happen to us at the end?

ONUCHOWGU: Life is a dancer; divinity is the drummer; destiny is the drum; the way the drum sounds is the way the dance step goes. We are all slaves of destiny and must be prepared to be shepherded by its premonitions. Whether it would end well or not the final drumming would tell.

AJANIGO: My lord, I think we can be consoled by the support we still receive from the town's people.

ONUCHOWGU: Ajanigo remember that it is not only the leaves that beautify a tree but also the branches that hold the leaves; if the branches die the leaves dry. The people's eyes in my administration are the ones revolting against me. When the chips are down, the people will stand by their eyes.

AJANIGO: My lord, why not call the Chief Priest and open up to him so as to get him to stand firmly behind us especially having denied been part of the plotters.

ONUCHOWGU: The rat being hunted by the cat adds to its misfortune if it runs to seek deliverance in the hands of the viper. Ogecha's face has never convinced me to believe in him.

AJANIGO: But as the mouthpiece of the gods, I think you should give him a chance my lord.

(*Omale enters escorted in by Aduku and both pay homage. Aduku leaves. Omale sits on the floor*)

OMALE: Your highness, I have come to honour your call.

ONUCHOWGU: Omale, does the fly become so well to do as to forsake the faeces?

OMALE: No my lord.

ONUCHOWGU: Then why has your cock stopped crowing at dawn?

OMALE: My lord; the distance of the thumb from the rest of the fingers does not mean they are no friends.

ONUCHOWGU: If you mean what you just said, why have you not been updating me?

OMALE: My lord; when a man is in the land of the living, he talks, but when he joins them in the land of the dead, the code of conduct of the cemetery demands absolute silence. Your highness, my abode has changed!

(*Onuchowgu and Ajanigo gaze at each other in surprise*)

ONUCHOWGU: You mean there is no fish for my kingfisher to eat in your river anymore?

OMALE: No more my lord.

ONUCHOWGU: (*disappointedly*) I can see. The cat has seen a rat; it has now decided to be quiet because it does not want to miss. Omale, when bile reveals itself from its hiding, he that must consume his meat free from bitterness must cast it away. Having you around is like having a basket for storage of water; it is as good as having no water storage. The time for you and I to path ways has come. One of us is now a prey and the other is a predator. A prey and a predator don't cohabit. Depart from me now lest I do to you what predators do their prey!

OMALE: Forgive me my lord. I am still on your side. There is nothing for me to say; that is why you have not been hearing from me.

ONUCHOWGU: (*aggressively*) you slapped a sleeping python on the face and you dare stand to plead when you have the chance to flee. Every moment more you spend with me now is provocative. Leave now lest I consume you!

OMALE: Please your highness; have mercy on your subject. I can't stand your wrath.

ONUCHOWGU: The tree that invokes the wrath of the thunder invokes doom! Guards!

(*Omale jumps up and hurries out*)

AJANIGO: My lord; this is unbelievable!

ONUCHOWGU: Ajanigo; the only palm tree that gives me wine in the jungle of fruitless trees is now dead. You can see now that my foes are multiplying! (*Enter Okpanachi and Anibe; pay homage*) My children; what is this that I am seeing: our teeth dwelll in the nose; our eyes now breathe; our mouths see; our hands now walk; our legs now put food in our noses; our land has gone up to replace the sky and we are now standing on our sky; how do we bring the situation back to normal?

OKPANACHI & ANIBE: (*gaze at each other confusedly*) we don't know my lord.

ONUCHOWGU: (*after a pause*) by the way, how was your surveillance? Is there anything new?

OKPANACHI: Father; the Chiefs met again today.

ONUCHOWGU: (*curiously*) and what was it all about this time around?

OKPANACHI: Father; they discussed the need to get the

support of the Assembly of Aneile elders after which they will constitute a powerful delegation of elders to proceed to Dekina to persuade the *Eje of Dekina* our District Head.

ONUCHOWGU: (*after a pause*) when did they plan to contact the Assembly of Elders?

OKPANACHI: They have not decided yet.

ANIBE: Though we suspect they later went ahead to have a closed door meeting in another venue which we could not locate. And we also believe that further decisions would have been taken on a lot of issues.

ONUCHOWGU: What do we do?

AJANIGO: My lord; I suggest you invite the Assembly of Elders first before they do.

ONUCHOWGU: And what do I tell them?

AJANIGO: My lord; you can intimate them about the ongoing conspiracy and advice them to act wisely when contacted by the Chiefs.

ONUCHOWGU: That may not be a wise decision.

AJANIGO: Why do you think so my lord?

ONUCHOWGU: They may misunderstand such a move.

AJANIGO: But it is more rewarding than silence my lord.

ONUCHOWGU: (*after a pause*) I shall give it a trial.

AJANIGO: That could be rewarding my lord.

OKPANACHI: Father; should we instruct the town crier to call for the meeting of the Elders in the palace immediately?

71

ONUCHOWGU: A hungry leopard does not roar when it tip toes to catch an antelope. The announcement of the town crier would arouse suspicion among the Chiefs and that would afford them more opportunity to heighten their conspiracy. I have a different approach.

OKPANACHI: What is it, father?

ONUCHOWGU: Okpanachi, go in and call Atuluku your brother while Anibe should go to Enemaku's house and invite him and his two sons Achimugu and Ainoko to join you. You will all go quietly to the houses of the elders of the land and intimate them of the development in my name and that I pray them to act wisely when contacted by the Chiefs. Let them also know that the gods and *ibegwu* our ancestors are watching. Tell them that the land is slippery and we all must tread it with caution. Is that understood?

OKPANACHI & ANIBE: Yes your highness.

ONUCHOWGU: Go now!

(*Exeunt Okpanachi and Anibe; lights fade out*)

ACT THREE SCENE FIVE

Chiefs celebrate. They entertain themselves with wine and exchange jokes. Hysterical laughter takes over the stage. Omale enters.

OMALE: (*surprised*) Chiefs of Aneile, who among you has his wife just put to bed?

CHIEF: (*hysterically*) All of us!!!

OMALE: Chiefs of Aneile, the cow has not only weaned her toothless calf but has forbidden it from ever coming close to her; how would the calf survive?

CHIEFS: Which is the cow that has chased its calf?

OMALE: The king chased me not only out of his palace but also out of his vicinity. I am sad about it.

EBILOMA: Why did he chase you out?

OMALE: He said the adored nightingale that sings melodious music to the delightfulness of its owner stands ejected from the owner's house the day it turns to an owl that hoots to terrify the owner's heart. Since I have nothing useful to offer him

ACT FOUR SCENE ONE

It is night in Aneile. Ajanigo sleeps deeply while Onuchowgu sits on his bed meditating. Upon realizing that he is not lying on the bed, she gets up and moves close to him.

AJANIGO: My lord, why are you not sleeping? (*No response*) my lord…

ONUCHOWGU: (*cuts in*) It is only a mad man who slumbers in a jungle overtaken by the hurricane.

AJANIGO: My lord, what is it again?

ONUCHOWGU: (*angrily*) woman, if a man's only house burns and he weeps, it is foolishness asking him why he has chosen to weep!

AJANIGO: (*feels embarrassed*) my dear husband, are you calling me a fool?

ONUCHOWGU: (*remorsefully*) I am sorry my wife. It is not my fault. A dry wood kept on hot embers is not hard to set ablaze at the slightest blow of wind. Forgive me my dear wife.

AJANIGO: That's alright my lord. I want you to always bear in mind that what follows the ugly dark cloud is a beautiful white sky. I know the gods and the ancestral spirits would someday bring a smile to our faces.

ONUCHOWGU: Ajanigo; you are a great wife. What scares me is that the thieves are already at the door of a house, yet the watchdog is not even grumbling let alone barks at the sight of the oncoming thieves; does that not signify an end to the treasures in the house? It seems as if the gods and the ancestral spirits are condoning what the chiefs are doing. They are still silent!

AJANIGO: (*after a pause*) I am also amazed at that. My lord, I have another suggestion.

ONUCHOWGU: What is it my wife?

AJANIGO: Why don't you send errands to Ayangba and Idah to seek divinations from the *Ifa* Priest and the Chief Priest of the Ancestral shrine respectively?

ONUCHOWGU: Ajanigo my dear wife, what the dog sees and does not bark at, the lion does not see it and roar at it. If our own gods find nothing wrong with what is happening, you don't expect the *Ifa* and the Ancestral deities to reach a different conclusion.

AJANIGO: You are right my lord. (*After a pause*) does that mean there is no positive end to this predicament?

ONUCHOWGU: The wound that would heal in time does not swell of pus when all antidotes have been exhausted.

AJANIGO: But why are the gods and the ancestral spirits doing this to us?

ONUCHOWGU: They have simply chosen to relate with us in the manner that it is done in the grave yard: no matter how the whirlwind rampages, the dead don't talk.

AJANIGO: My lord, do you suggest we run away?

ONUCHOWGU: It is more honourable for a man beaten by rain in the desert to stay calmly and suffer the lashes of the rain meekly; for what respite does he get by running all day seeking refuge in a land of no shelter?

AJANIGO: (*sobs*) gods of our ancestors why? Our ancestral spirits why? What have we done to deserve all these?

ONUCHOWGU: (*pacifies her*) Ajanigo, if tears could bring solutions to problems, then the world we are would have been flooded with oceans of tears of the afflicted; but it cannot. It only weakens us the more. Like you earlier said behind every dark cloud is a beautiful white sky. Let us wait and see if our own destiny would believe in that order. Weep no more woman.

(*Onuchowgu helps her to lie back on her pillow; lights fade out*)

ACT FOUR SCENE TWO

The Elders of the land have gathered at the village square, all seated. The Chiefs enter one after the other and set to address them.

EBILOMA: Elders of Aneile we greet you all!

ELDERS: We greet you too!!!

EBILOMA: Elders of our land, no one becomes great by farming with borrowed tools. We have endured enough of irritating food in our stomachs; it is time to vomit them to regain our health. We have come to confirm the rumour that has been spreading like wild fire across the land for sometimes now. The reign of Onuchowgu must be brought to an end as a matter of urgency!

FIRST ELDER: Chief Ebiloma, like you said, none of us is ignorant of your evil plot against the king. We want to know why you have suddenly begun to revolt against a man so much loved by Aneile people.

THE REST ELDERS: Yes we want to know!!!

EBILOMA: Thank you elders of our land; some of you have been told that some evil chiefs are revolting against the king but that is not true. If there is nothing heating its buttock hard, the baby in the womb of the pot does cry out in pains.

SECOND ELDER: What is it? We want to know!

THE REST ELDERS: Yes we want to know now!!!

ABALAKA: Be patient Elders. It takes caution to consume a bony fish.

THIRD ELDER: (*aggressively*) don't preach caution to us! We are talking about a king whose type we have never had in this land. His father took this land from the doldrums of decadence and total collapse to a citadel of prosperity. The son came and has been treading the path of his father. He has moved ahead of his father with wiser and more people-oriented decisions. Today Aneile is one of the most prosperous lands in the entire Igala Kingdom thanks to Onuchowgu and his father. How come you are now rewarding him by washing his face with your hands full of pepper?

THE REST OF ELDERS: Yes tell us now!!!

OCHEJA: Elders of our land, you may be right to believe that the king and his father have liberated our land from poverty and misfortune but one thing you must all bear in mind is that no matter how impressive your barber has shaved your head, you do not reward his expertise by allowing him to behead you!

ELDERS: How do you mean?!!!

(*Elders murmur in expression of anger*)

EBILOMA: Calm down elders of Aneile. The territorial war engaged in by the Agama lizard is not for his interest alone;

he is fighting for his generations yet unborn. Be calm, I shall let you know everything you want to know.

ELDERS: Let us know now!!!

EBILOMA: Like you all know, Ilemona, the King's father was a slave hunter from Abejukolo who emerged as king because he was among the warriors that saved Aneile in the battle against Ujayan.

ELDERS: And what about that?!!!

EBILOMA: Obaje, the Chief Priest's brother as you all know was the *Akogwu* – Commander of Aneile Army. He fought along Edime my father and Ilemona the King's father. When Aneile army seemed to be overwhelmed by Ujayan warriors, our men including Ilemona ran away one after the other from the battle field leaving behind only Obaje. When Ilemona noticed that Obaje was not among the escaped warriors, he summoned courage and ran back to the battle field where he met him single-handedly destroying Ujayan army. He hid himself and watched Obaje completely destroyed the enemies. Obaje whose wife and children were in *Agojeeju* proceeded there from the battle field to bring them back to Aneile but before he came back, Ilemona who happened to be the highest ranked warrior in the absence of Obaje and Edime my father, claimed to be single-handedly behind the victory. The town's people and elders were blindfolded by his lies and in conspiracy with the then Chief Priest Ukpahiu, he was crowned King of Ancile. In order to avert the wrath of the gods and our ancestral spirits and establish his generation as kings of Aneile, Ukpahiu made forbidden sacrifices to drive away the potency of the gods and the ancestral spirits. Hence the gods and ancestors of Aneile have long deserted this land.

ELDERS: (*not convinced*) lies!!! Nothing but lies!!!

FOURTH ELDER: We need proof!

THE REST ELDERS: Yes we need proofs!!!

EBILOMA: Ogecha the Chief Priest can testify!

(*Ogecha enters*)

ELDERS: (*shocked*) what, the Chief Priest?!!!

(*Elders murmur noisily*)

IDACHABA: Elders of our land calm down and listen.

FIFTH ELDER: Wise one, are the Chiefs telling us the truth?

OGECHA: Elders of our land; as you all know; the concussion of bitter herbs does not taste well to swallow, but if a sick man must gain relief, he must let go the fear of a resentful taste. What you have just heard is the whole truth. There is no iota of lie in it. If fishes begin to run out of water, let no other tenant of the river stay behind; for calamity looms ahead. I hereby corroborate and confirm all the chiefs have told you and I expect all of you to join us in this crusade to fight for what belong to our people; for posterity will blame us if this land suffers the irredeemable consequences of allowing this state of affairs to continue.

ELDERS: You mean we should believe this people?!!!

OGECHA: Elders of Aneile, if the lizard suddenly begins to chase you, something else is after it; do not run for the lizard but run for that thing that chases the lizard. Don't believe the story because you don't trust the chiefs but think of the consequences of not believing what they are saying and believe them.

(*There is confusion among the elders as arguments, comments, murmurs and side talks take over the stage*)

EBILOMA: Attention! Attention Elders of our land. (*Noise dies down*) you have all heard the hidden truth now. It has been like a baby python caught and kept under a basket and now it has outgrown the basket and has run out into our street. If we don't make urgent effort to kill it, we may pay dearly for that negligence.

SIXTH ELDER: Why didn't you tell us all these before the coronation of Onuchowgu?

THE REST ELDERS: Yes, why?!!!

EBILOMA: Elders of our land, the truth was hidden from you because the king pleaded with us to keep it secret.

SEVENTH ELDER: You mean the king himself knows the truth?

EBILOMA: He knows everything.

EIGHT ELDER: But why have you decided to betray him now?

(*The rest elders gesticulate in support of the question*)

EBILOMA: The Priest of Ifa Oracle in Ayangba visited and told Elder Ogecha that divination revealed that there would be deadly consequences should we continue to hide the truth from the people. The Priest also warned that urgent steps must be taken to redress the situation before the gods and the ancestral spirits strike.

NINETH ELDER: What do you want us to do now?

EBILOMA: That is why we have come to you for deliberation.

TENTH ELDER: Well, it is very simple. We elders of this land are still loyal to King Onuchowgu. As custom and tradition demand, we would have to refer this controversy to the District Head in Dekina. We shall wait for the resolution of the district head before we know what next to do. My fellow elders, have I spoken your minds?

THE REST ELDERS: Well spoken!!!

EBILOMA: That decision is okay by us. We shall constitute a delegation made up of Chiefs and Elders of Aneile to proceed to Dekina as soon as possible. Is that okay with you elders?

ELDERS: It is in order!!!

EBILOMA: Thank you elders for coming. We shall convene again as soon as the delegation returns from Dekina.

(*Elders murmur as they disperse one after the other, some expressing surprise while others express disappointment*)

ACT FOUR SCENE THREE

Onuchowgu sits in his palace; his younger son Atuluku stands beside him with Onuchowgu's hand about him. They converse in silent tone. Rush in Anibe and Enemaku gasping for breath and manage to pay homage.

ANIBE: Your high…..ness……., your…….hi….

ONUCHOWGU: (*shocked and stands on his feet*) what is it Anibe?

ANIBE: (*still gasping for breath*) your high…ness; the worst volcano has erupted! Your people are all over the town protesting against your kingship. Soon they will be here. In fact, your chiefs are closer than the town's people and they have vowed to force you out of the palace as soon as they get here!

The guards stand firmly at alert facing the entrance direction.

ATULUKU: (*panic-stricken*) what!

ONUCHOWGU: (*laughs mildly expressing sarcasm*) the hanging and dangling rock of calamity has finally crashed on Aneile. What a celebration of misfortune!

ENEMAKU: Your highness, a man who is being chased by the hyena does not pause to catch fun when the hyena is at a close step. The evil men are approaching your palace!

ONUCHOWGU: (*calmly*) Enemaku my friend, the antelope that has been chased far does not express shock when the hunter draws near. It is no longer of any use preaching caution to a man whose legs have already given way on a slippery ground. The grass cutter that runs with a trap on its legs only adds to its misfortune. There is nothing anymore for us to do at this stage.

ENEMAKU: Please your highness, let us run away and seek refuge in the neighbouring village.

ONUCHOWGU: Enemaku, no matter how severe the earthquake terrorizes the earth, the land does not run away.

ANIBE: Your highness, please do something before it is late.

ONUCHOWGU: What do you expect the antelope to do when its abdomen is already in the mouth of the python?!

THE CHIEF GUARD: Your highness, command that I mobilize the palace guards to attack them.

ONUCHOWGU: When fire consumes a thatched house, another thatched house does not go to put out the fire lest both fall victims! This is the battle of the marauding army of deadly shoulder ants against the maggots; no amount of bravery can deliver the maggots from facing calamity.

CHIEF GUARD: But my lord, are you by any means suggesting that we should fold our arms and watch this people come here to disrespect your authority and person?

ONUCHOWGU: Guard, a leper's fist does not scare even a child! These people are coming in great numbers against a dozen of you. There is nothing you can do to scare them away. Leave me and them to sort out ourselves in the manner they want it.

(*Rush in Ajanigo and Okpanachi gasping for breath*)

AJANIGO: My lord, what are we still doing in the palace?

ONUCHOWGU: Ajanigo, why are you asking a bird what it is doing in its own nest?

OKPANACHI: But father this people are already close to the entrance of the palace!

ONUCHOWGU: Then what do you want me to do?

AJANIGO: My lord let us run away before it is too late.

ENEMAKU: That is exactly what I have been telling the King.

OKPANACHI & ATULUKU: Yes father, let us run away now!!

ONUCHOWGU: My people, no matter how violent the thunder explodes, the sky does not abdicates its position of authority. Besides, the lion is not called the king of the jungle because he roars but because he stands to dare where other animals start to run. Moreover, I was not born a chicken so why would I have the heart of a chicken and begin to run at the sight of shadows?

AJANIGO: So what do we do now my lord?

ONUCHOWGU: When the dry wood burns, the land that carries it bears the pain with it. Stay by me and bear with me whatever may happen to me.

(*Ogecha, Ebiloma, Ocheja, Abalaka, Idachaba and Omale; all*

CHORUS: *Ayenla o ayenla, ichonu we che ayenla ---- [donkey, donkey you are not a king]*

ROYAL BARD: Great people of Aneile, the King greets you!

TOWN'S PEOPLE: He is no longer our king!!!

[*Murmurs and noise among the town's people take over the stage and gradually die down*]

ONUCHOWGU: People of Aneile, why is it that it is only in this land that dogs grow horns, cows lay eggs, mosquitoes grow moustache and chickens produce venoms?!

TOWN'S PEOPLE: You are a liar!!!

ONE CITIZEN: Your highness, we have come to tell you to vacate our throne immediately. In case you are not aware, our decision was not made without a reason because you know how much we loved you. When we were told how your father with the help of the late Chief Priest and some elders of this land most of whom are now late plotted and succeeded in establishing the ruling dynasty of slaves in this land, we didn't believe them. We asked your chiefs for proofs. They called the Assembly of elders, they came and they testified. Still we did not believe them and we asked for further proof. They proceeded to Dekina and came back with a finding that all the allegations were true. Yet we did not believe and they invited Ogecha the mouthpiece of the gods and that was it. What further proof do we need that could be better than the corroboration of the mouthpiece of the gods? Consequently, we have come to tell you to vacate our throne with immediate effect! (*Turns to the crowd*) My people have I spoken your minds?!

TOWN'S PEOPLE: Yes!!! Well spoken!!! Leave now!!!

ONUCHOWGU: People of Aneile I am shocked to my

96

marrow that you do not understand that when a witch stands trial in a court of justice against a godly man and the devil is invited to ascertain the guilt or innocence of both parties, you do not expect the devil to tell you that the witch is guilty and the godly man is innocent. Have you not realized that the corroborative evidence you are relying on to hang a good man are all coming out from the mouths of men who have been possessed by demonic spirits?!

TOWN'S PEOPLE: We have made up our minds!!!

ONUCHOWGU: What amazes me most is the fact that it is only in this land that a man is ever condemned unheard. Two groups are disputing over an issue and you are making a decision solely on the evidence of one group against the other group. What a slaughter of justice! Have I ever judged any of you in that manner?!

ANOTHER CITIZEN: We wanted to give you an audience but we were further provoked when we were further told that your father and Ukpahiu the late Chief Priest imported foreign gods from Yoruba, Nupe, Idoma, Igbo and Jukun lands to replace our gods which made our gods depart us and turned their backs on us. We were also told how the late Chief Priest fed the foreign gods with abominable sacrifices to render them impotent. We wouldn't have believed all these if the silence of the gods for so many moons now in spite the looming calamity in the land has not validated the allegations!

ONUCHOWGU: (*flabbergasted*) you mean they told you all these?!

TOWN'S PEOPLE: Yes the good people did!!!

ONUCHOWGU: And you believe them?!

TOWN'S PEOPLE: Stop wasting our time!!!

allowing the evil men to appoint a representative to accompany him.

ONUCHOWGU: They would not believe us if the decision favours us. Besides, it was their idea that both parties should be represented and I concurred in the interest of justice and fair play.

(*Enter Aduku*)

ANIBE: My lord here he comes.

(*Aduku pays homage*)

ONUCHOWGU: Aduku you are welcome. Your late arrival scared us. The hooting of the owl or the melody of the nightingale, which one do you have for us?

ADUKU: My lord, Atta greets you.

ONUCHOWGU: Thank you.

ADUKU: The Achadu greets you too.

ONUCHOWGU: (*furiously*) Aduku you waste my time! A man with fish bone in his throat does not spare time to listen to fables. What is the news?!

ADUKU: (*timidly*) Atta said your time is off!

(*Everybody is shocked*)

ONUCHOWGU: What! No! A cat does not give birth to a kitten and nurture the puppy of a dog. This is not true!

ENEMAKU: Aduku, tell us it is not true.

ADUKU: It is true.

AJANIGO: No, it can't be true.

OKPANACHI: That my father's reign on the throne is over?

ADUKU: Yes my prince.

EJURA: This is impossible.

AJANIGO: Where is the representative of the Chiefs and elders that went with you?

ADUKU: My queen, he has gone to deliver the message to the chiefs and elders.

AJANIGO: My lord, it is all over. Let's leave immediately.

ONUCHOWGU: Aduku, I hope you know that if a man consumes from the locust bean temporarily kept in his care, his mouth will smell when he gives account to the owner.

ADUKU: My lord, I am confused.

ENEMAKU: Aduku, are you giving us the true message you are sent or have those serpents changed the honey to poison in your hands?

ADUKU: The gods bear me witness.

ONUCHOWGU: Then I believe you. But it leaves so much to be desired to hear that the mane of a lion withers away when the lion still lives.

(*Everybody looks down cast; Okpanachi and Atuluku sob while Ajanigo and Ejura try to hold their own tears as they pacify them*)

ENEMAKU: My lord, I still believe that the lioness does not throw away her cub in exchange for a baby elephant simply because the baby elephant is more robust.

ONUCHOWGU: I believe exactly the same thing too. But he

ACT FIVE SCENE ONE

Ogecha is now king. The chiefs are waiting. The royal bard enters and awaits his arrival. He enters.

ROYAL BARD: The king of kings; the lion that roars to upturn the foundation of the earth; the mighty tree that instills great fear in the heart of the hurricane. You are the king of man and spirits whose names scare even the demons. *Onujaaashi.*

(*Everybody pays homage. Exit the royal bard*)

OGECHA: The living spirits of Aneile, I greet you.

CHIEFS: We greet you too, your highness.

OGECHA: May I once again thank you for selecting me as your king and for all the support you have so far given to me and I hope to continue enjoying such support and cooperation. May I also emphatically pronounce that I am in full support of your arrangement of having four ruling houses belonging to the four of you among which the throne of this land shall be rotated after my reign and also the choice of Omale as the Head of the Kingmakers of Aneile. I thank you all. In fact, you are more than chiefs to me. That is why I refer to you as the living spirits of Aneile. May we continue to enjoy the comfort of power and authority in this land and beyond.

EBILOMA: Your highness, on behalf of myself and my colleagues, I thank you too for the confidence you repose in us. I also want to thank you for not letting us down when we needed you most. I am assuring you of our continuous alluring support and cooperation during your reign. (*Turns to his fellow chiefs*) My fellow chiefs, have I spoken your minds?

CHIEFS: Well spoken.

OGECHA: Thank you the living spirits of Aneile. Now back to the business of the day. What is it that I hear about Ukwumonu?

EBILOMA: My lord, Ukwumonu is planning rebellion against us.

OGECHA: Why?

EBILOMA: It is in respect of the plots of land we took from him and others.

OGECHA: Does he not know that in the jungle there is nothing the herbivores can do about the dominance and oppression of the carnivores? Nature has made it so.

IDACHABA: Your highness, it is a serious matter. Information reaching us is to the effect that Ukwumonu has mobilized all his counterparts along with their families and they will soon stage a violent protest against us.

OGECHA: So what do you suggest we do?

OCHEJA: Your highness, the finger that wrestles with the knife pays with its own blood. Let's kill him to scare away others!

OGECHA: Living spirits of Aneile, does anyone has any objection?

EBILOMA: The egg that wants to strike the rock deserves no pity from the rock. It is a perfect suggestion.

ABALAKA: Since foolishness has pushed the winged termite to turn the tongue of the toad to a dancing floor, it has to pay the price of going down to mother-earth as the excrement of the toad. There is no objection my lord.

IDACHABA: The yam flour that attempts to embarrass the wind would waste. Let him pay the price for his folly.

OGECHA: Ocheja, I give you that assignment. Ensure that it is done in a clean way to avoid any linkage to the palace.

EBILOMA: Your highness, there is no better choice in the task of bone crushing than the hyena. He is a specialist in that regard.

OCHEJA: (*smiles*) my lord, you will surely not be disappointed.

OGECHA: Now to the unresolved issue of the position of Chief Priest, how do we go about it?

ABALAKA: Your highness, we seek to rely on your expert opinion.

THE REST CHIEFS: (*simultaneously*) precisely.

OGECHA: Then you have it! First and foremost, I have made some sacrifices to appease the gods and the ancestral spirits for not waiting for them to speak before doing what we did. As it is now, there is no cause for alarm. As regards the issue of the office of the Chief Priest, I am thinking of grooming my eldest son for the job. But for now, while he remains an apprentice under me, I shall still have charge of the shrine.

CHIEFS: That is perfect!!

OGECHA: Is there any issue worthy of discussing before we adjourn today's sitting?

IDACHABA: (*after some silence in the house*) my lord, I think we should also settle the issue of tributes now.

OGECHA: I agree with you. So what do you suggest we do about it?

IDACHABA: Every family should be made to bring annual tributes as against the usual optional few. Or my fellow chiefs, what do you think?

CHIEFS: Good idea.

EBILOMA: The tributes should be two – third of annual harvest of each farmer.

ABALAKA: And should be subject to constant review by this council.

OCHEJA: Severe punishment should be melted on every defaulter.

OGECHA: So be it! Idachaba, you shall be in charge of matters involving tributes.

IDACHABA: It shall be diligently done my lord.

OGECHA: Ocheja, all matters relating to the opposition shall now be handled by you.

OCHEJA: Your wish is my command my lord.

OGECHA: Abalaka, you will henceforth handle issues relating to festivals and ceremonies.

ABALAKA: It is an honour my lord.

OGECHA: Ebiloma, matters relating to lands and forestry shall be within your exclusive powers.

EBILOMA: I am always at your service my lord.

OGECHA: Whenever you deem it necessary, do not forget to employ the services of Omale.

CHIEFS: That will be done your highness.

OGECHA: The living spirits of Aneile, I thank you all for your wise deliberations and decisions. This sitting stands adjourned till the next appearance of the moon subject to individual reports and emergencies.

CHIEFS: Thank you your highness.

Lights fade out.

ACT FIVE SCENE TWO

Three men are on their way to the farm. Each of them has a hoe, a cutlass and a basket. They walk side by side and stop to engage in passionate conversation.

FIRST MAN: I find it difficult to imagine that all these evils are befalling our land after all the prosperity we have enjoyed.

SECOND MAN: Our sorrow began the day Onuchowgu left this land.

THIRD MAN: Each time I remember that I was not part of those who made the evil decision to dethrone him, I feel proud of myself.

FIRST MAN: Likewise me.

SECOND MAN: And me too.

THIRD MAN: Can you imagine the sort of draconian laws the king and his chiefs are imposing on us.

FIRST MAN: It leaves so much to be desired that Ogecha of

ACT FIVE SCENE THREE

There is a loud noise behind the stage. In the palace, the chiefs are eagerly waiting for the arrival of Ogecha. He enters. The chiefs pay homage in a hurry. The backstage noise dies down.

OGECHA: My chiefs what is it that I am hearing in town?

EBILOMA: My lord, Aneile is boiling in calamities!

OGECHA: What is happening?

EBILOMA: Our people are dying of mysterious ailments!

OCHEJA: Pregnant women are dying during labour!

IDACHABA: Hundreds of infants have been attacked and killed by strange convulsions!

ABALAKA: A large number of our able-bodied men are now victims of strange and deadly chicken pox, small pox and measles!

OGECHA: (*shocked*) what!

EBILOMA: That is not all your highness. Report reaching us from our farmers is that our crops are drying up in spite the heavy down pour.

OCHEJA: And very soon we may all die of starvation!

OGECHA: (*gets up furiously*) what is happening in Aneile?!

ABALAKA: My lord, it seems the gods are on vengeance mission.

OGECHA: But I have performed several appeasement sacrifices to them.

IDACHABA: My lord; may be they did not accept the sacrifices.

OGECHA: But that is unusual.

EBILOMA: That is why they are gods. Their ways are mysterious.

OGECHA: What do we do now?

EBILOMA: My lord, you need to address your people, we have to express our condolence to the bereaved and empathize with the afflicted.

ABALAKA: And also raise their hope of an urgent remedy.

OCHEJA: And that has to be done immediately to prevent possible aggression and attack by the people.

OGECHA: Would that be enough?

OCHEJA: My lord; that would be a starting point. After then, I suggest we hold an emergency meeting to find a way out of the calamity.

OGECHA: I think you are right. Guard! (*Guard runs in and*

pays homage) tell the town crier to inform the town's people to gather at the village square immediately to meet me.

GUARD: Consider it done your highness. (*Runs out*)

Background noise grows louder. Lights fade out.

ACT FIVE SCENE FOUR

There is war drumming at the background; the Chiefs rush into the palace together.

OGECHA: My chiefs what is the matter?

EBILOMA: My lord, the foundations of our houses are crumbling; the voracious mouth of the land is wide open to swallow us!

OGECHA: What is happening?

EBILOMA: Your people are revolting!

OCHEJA: They are trooping towards the palace like mad dogs on loose!

IDACHABA: They are all armed to the teeth!

ABALAKA: This palace will embrace its foundation should they be allowed to get here!

OGECHA: (*shocked*) what! Why are they doing this? Have I not addressed and calmed them down?

EBILOMA: My lord, they said they no longer have confidence in your administration.

IDACHABA: And they call for an immediate change of hand!

OGECHA: (*gets up furiously*) how dare! What gave the goat the audacity to challenge the authority of its owner?

ABALAKA: My lord, what do we do?

OGECHA: It is simple; the yam stem that seeks to bring down the farm owner shall be taught an unforgettable lesson by the sharp edge of the farmer's matchet. Ocheja!

OCHEJA: Yes your highness.

OGECHA: Summon Akogwu, the Commander of Aneile Warriors; let him assemble all the warriors and the town's armory and go right now into the town. Whoever dares to raise a voice or make attempt to demonstrate should be brought down to join his ancestors in the pool of his own blood!

OCHEJA: Consider it done your highness.

War drumming increases at the background. Lights fade out.

ACT FIVE SCENE FIVE

At the village square; a group of armed men sing and dance to the drumming at the background. They carelessly brandish their weapons and yells.

FIRST MAN: (*steps out from the crowd*) calm down great men of Aneile! (*Noise dies down slowly*) calm down. This is a fight for our existence as a people. We must be prepared to live or die. Are we all battle ready?

ALL: Yes!!!

SECOND MAN: (*steps out of the crowd*) great men of Aneile; we are chickens whose brains were suddenly taken over by folly and has led us to choose hyenas as our rulers; now our houses are the pots of soups where we are being cooked by calamities. What a tragedy!

CROWD: Tragedy indeed!!!

(*Second man rejoins the crowd*)

THIRD MAN: (*steps out of the crowd*) we have sent our roofs packing; now our houses have been exposed to heavy

ACT SIX SCENE ONE

There is drumming and singing of war song at the background. At the palace; Ogecha enters and sits. The Chiefs rush in falling on one another in confusion. The backstage singing and drumming die down slowly.

OGECHA: (*frightened and jumps up*) Ebiloma, Ocheja, Abalaka, Idachaba, what is happening again?!

EBILOMA: (*regains composure*) your highness, some nearby villages have sent their troops and amoury to aid the rebels in kicking us out of power. The alien troops have started moving into Aneile through our borders north, south, east and west. In fact more lands are still threatening to send their troops to help the rebels dethrone you if you don't voluntarily abdicate the throne in few days!

OGECHA: What! Are they out of their minds?!

EBILOMA: To add insult to injury, all sojourners of Aneile have taken refuge in neighbouring lands while some have been recalled home by their rulers to avoid been hit by any weapon.

OCHEJA: My lord, the actions of the rebels have been approved far and near and in no long a time the hunter shall become the hunted.

EBILOMA: That is what we are already! The rebels and their foreign allies are everywhere in town wrecking havoc on whoever and whatever they perceive belong to us.

OGECHA: So, what do we do?

IDACHABA: We have to fight on.

ABALAKA: More youths should be recruited into the town's army.

EBILOMA: Where are the youths to recruit when every one of them has taken up arm against the kingdom?

OGECHA: What are our warriors doing Ocheja?

OCHEJA: My lord, the more the warriors kill, the more the rebels grow in numbers. Their army is almost insurmountable!

IDACHABA: It is a rare kind of revolution!

ABALAKA: Every one of them is fighting like a wounded lion!

OGECHA: What does this portend, spirits of Aneile?

EBILOMA: Calamity!

OGECHA: How do we survive it?

IDACHABA: To survive we need to revive our efforts at the battlefront.

ABALAKA: It is not the number of our warriors and weapons that would determine our victory but the strength of the warriors behind the weapons we wield. The remaining of our men need to fight with winning minds otherwise we are doomed!

OGECHA: (*calling*) spirits of Aneile!

CHIEFS: Yes your highness.

OGECHA: Contact the warriors, raise their morale and urge them to fight with winning minds. Tell them not to be intimidated by the number of the opposition but be energized by the greater rewards their victory stands to offer them. Let them know that we are all in for calamity should the rebels take over the land. Go now and carry out my command!

CHIEFS: (*set to leave*) consider it done your highness.

War drumming and singing restart at the background. Lights fade out.

ACT SIX SCENE TWO

At the village square; tension is high as Town's people attempt to lynch King Ogecha and his chiefs but prevented by a handful of lion-hearted guards. There are corpses and sick men lying in front of their relatives. Wailing and crying make the stage noisy. Ogecha peeps through the shield around him. A man comes forward to calm them down and address them.

ONE CITIZEN: Your highness; look at our people (*pointing at the lying corpses and sick men*) corpses and sick bodies of innocent sons and daughters of Aneile crying and begging for justice. Back there in our respective houses are helpless bodies of laboring mothers and infants lying and awaiting burials. How many more of us will go your highness?! Instead of finding solution to our problem, you sent a killer squad after us to kill and maim our people for daring to raise our voices against your oppression and insensitivity!

ANOTHER CITIZEN: Your highness, we are in the wet season yet no water to sustain our crops. There is heavy downpour yet our farms are drying up. A strange epidemic has taken over our land. Our sons are dying. Our daughters are wasting. Our mothers are falling. Our fathers are going down. Friends are no more. Brothers and sisters we have all lost. Men and women are victims. Our trees are collapsing. Our buildings are crumbling and even our animals are not spared. Our houses have become the firewood upon which we are being roasted alive by calamity. What have we done your highness?! (*Bursts into tears and other town's people do the same*)

OGECHA: (*struggles for words and manages to clear his throat*) my people. I sympathize with all of you. For those who have lost their beloved ones, please accept my condolences. Bury your dead and weep no more. I want you to know that we are like a fowl with a broken leg whose death never comes by the injury it carries about; we shall overcome this calamity.

A FEMALE CITIZEN: When? Is it after we have all been consumed by misfortune that we shall overcome? Tell us your highness! (*Bursts into tears and some close by fellow pacify her*).

A MALE CITIZEN: Your highness, we shall not leave here today until you voluntarily abdicate our throne and go into exile or we strike you dead!

TOWN'S PEOPLE: Yes!!!

(*An old man dressed in white rob and adorned with charms enters. He holds a scepter. The sight of him distracts the attention of everybody. He is recognized by Ogecha and the chiefs as Atebo*)

OGECHA: Atebo!

ATEBO: (*furiously*) don't even dare repeat that name again!

CHIEFS: The Custodian of the Royal Ancestral Shrine, we greet you.

ATEBO: (*still furious*) your greetings are evil! Hold them to yourselves! (*Faces the crowd*) People of Aneile, can you see what folly has done to you? I have never seen a people so senseless and stupid as you. Your case is like that of a moron of a man who puts up his head for roasting simply because he discovers a louse in it. How dare you! Why have you forgotten that no matter the size of a fish, it never controls the direction the river flows? Why would you think mere mortals would make better judgments than the immortals? Why did you allow these evil men take over the positions of the gods and the ancestral spirits in this land? (*There is sobriety among the crowd; some placing their hands on their chests and some on their heads as expressions of regrets*) you have slapped the gods and the ancestral spirits on their faces and the consequences are unimaginable. *Anjenu* is angry! *Ikpakachi* is aggrieved! *Ichekpa* is offended! *Iyama* cries for revenge! *Afu* is ready to strike! *Ogba* is furious! *Erane* breathes vengeance fire! *Ibegwus* threaten to vomit more calamities! What you have seen so far is still the gathering of the cloud; the tempestuous rain is still to come. By the time the gods and the ancestral spirits are through with you, the fallen walls of Aneile will be used by other lands to tell the tale of a land which once lived and fallen by the folly and evil of its people! (*The crowd panic*)

A MALE CITIZEN: (*prostrates*) wise one, have pity on us. We know we have overstepped our boundaries. We were misled by these men. We di….

ATEBO: (*cuts in aggressively*) shut up! Even a drunken antelope would not allow anyone to trick it to go and shave the mane of a sleeping lion. How dare you!

ANOTHER MALE CITIZEN: Wise one, it was the mouthpiece of the gods (*points at Ogecha*) that made us believe that the allegations leveled by chiefs against the gods, the ancestral spirits, king Onuchowgu and his father are true and

ACT SEVEN SCENE ONE

Three youths have been mandated to look for Onuchowgu.
They stop on their way to have some conversation.

FIRST YOUTH: Comrades which path do we take from here?

SECOND YOUTH: Let's take Egume road and proceed through Ankpa forest to Iyen just a few miles to Adoka.

THIRD YOUTH: I think I agree with that. It seems to be the easiest way to for us.

FIRST YOUTH: But why did the king choose to stay in Adoka, an Idoma land rather than our numerous Igala cities and towns?

SECOND YOUTH: My brother, wherever a man receives a hearty welcome is where he chooses as home. You know Adoka people are very hospitable and loving people. They have a way of making you disown your place of origin with their hospitality.

THIRD YOUTH: Besides, history has it that the king's great grandmother is from Adoka.

FIRST YOUTH: No wonder.

SECOND YOUTH: Moreover, the king felt betrayed by his Igala brothers and would prefer to find solace in the bosom of another people and Adoka is just a perfect place for that.

FIRST YOUTH: It is heart rending to think of the ruthless manner the great king Onuchowgu was dethroned and sent packing from Aneile.

SECOND YOUTH: It was when Ogecha the Chief Priest corroborated the allegations of the chiefs that my father and I threw our support behind them.

THIRD YOUTH: Mine was when the district head ruled in favour of the chiefs.

FIRST YOUTH: My family did not believe the allegations until Aduku returned from Idah and said that the Atta's Court ruled in favour of the Chiefs.

SECOND YOUTH: Thanks to the gods and the ancestral spirits, Aduku is now reaping the fruits of his evil.

THIRD YOUTH: But the king should have sent another person to proceed to Idah to confirm the ruling of Atta's Court.

FIRST YOUTH: The king had no reason to doubt a man that has been working for him for more than a decade.

SECOND YOUTH: Moreover, the evil men would still have found their way to force the second person to join them or even eliminate him if he refuses.

FIRST YOUTH: Those men are evil incarnate!

SECOND YOUTH: Their types are not worthy of having in any land.

THIRD YOUTH: Comrades, our elders say that a man who is sent to deliver hot embers with bare hands does not stand on his way to chat with anyone – not even a missing friend long sought after. We have been saddled with the arduous task of bringing back the king within seven days. A day is already smiling away from us and we are still here doing nothing.

FIRST YOUTH: Yes, you are right. Comrades, let's go! (*Exeunt*)

ACT SEVEN SCENE TWO

It is night and darkness covers the stage as the three youths arrive at Adoka's border with Igala land.

FIRST YOUTH: Comrades, thanks to the gods, we have made it to Adoka.

SECOND YOUTH: It is better we rest here and proceed at dawn.

(*Some noise could be heard at a distance*)

THIRD YOUTH: Comrades, are you not hearing what am hearing?

THE REST YOUTH: And what are you hearing?

THIRD YOUTH: Unfamiliar voices up there.

(*They become attentive and could hear the voices clearly*)

FIRST YOUTH: Those must be the voices of hunters from Adoka.

SECOND YOUTH: But hunters don't make noise while hunting you know.

THIRD YOUTH: They do only when they are resting.

FIRST YOUTH: But not without a blazing fire in front of them.

SECOND YOUTH: Comrades, how could we predict the sex of a chick from a distance? Why don't we simply move down the forest to find out what is there?

THIRD YOUTH: Then let's go comrades.

They walk down the stage. Lights fade out and shine on two middle age men dressed as hunters sitting and facing each other with a burning fire in between them. The three youths find them.

YOUTHS: Elders we greet you.

HUNTERS: (*surprised*) Young men what are you doing in this deadly jungle?

FIRST YOUTH: Elders, we seek Onuchowgu the king of Aneile.

FIRST HUNTER: In this deadly forest?

SECOND HUNTER: By this time of the night?

FIRST HUNTER: By the way, is he missing??

SECOND YOUTH: Elders it is a long story.

SECOND HUNTER: We are not asking you to tell us stories. As you can see we are hunters on a business of hunting. There is no part of our schedule of duty that relates to storytelling. So, we have no time to listen to your stories.

FIRST HUNTER: In brief, tell us why you are looking for your king.

(*The three youths whisper to one another*)

THIRD YOUTH: Elders we are from Aneile, a distant but friendly neighbor of Adoka. Some chiefs conspired and illegally dethroned our king and enthroned themselves. As a result, the gods and the ancestral spirits were provoked and have unleashed terror on the land. They have given us seven days ultimatum within which to bring him back to the throne of Aneile or we face extinction!

FIRST YOUTH: Information reached us that the king now resides here in Adoka.

SECOND HUNTER: We know the story more than you have told us. The whole world is disappointed in all of you for what you did.

SECOND YOUTH: It was the chiefs that conspired and dethroned him.

FIRST HUNTER: Shut up! Did you people not support them?

THIRD YOUTH: They misled us.

SECOND HUNTER: If the ducks are jumping into the river and urging the hens to do the same, why would the hens not be wise enough to know that their own feathers are allergic to water before obeying the clarion call?

YOUTHS: We accept our mistakes.

HUNTERS: (*rhetorically*) do you have an option?

(*Hunters come together and whisper in low tones*)

FIRST HUNTER: Well, we have resolved not to behave like Aneile that medicates a man stung by scorpion with the venom of a viper. We shall help you.

YOUTHS: (*excitedly*) thank you elders.

SECOND HUNTER: Although we are hunters from Ankpa and not Adoka but we know where your king resides. We intend to liaise with our fellow hunters from Adoka to take you to where he is.

YOUTHS: Elders, we can't thank you enough.

FIRST HUNTER: Come over here (*points at a free space*) and relax. When it is dawn, we shall proceed to Adoka.

Lights fade out.

ACT SEVEN SCENE THREE

Onuchowgu sits and chats with the whole of his family including Enemaku, his wife and son.

THE MAN: (*pays homage*) your highness, some youths are here to see you.

ONUCHOWGU: Youths? Where are they coming from?

THE MAN: They brought a message for you from Aneile.

(*Everybody becomes curious and gesticulates in surprise*)

ONUCHOWGU: Let them in. (*The three youths are led in. They pay homage and remain squatting*) sons of Aneile; the comb of the cock suffers the onslaught of flies only in the day time but when he takes residence under the bosom of the night, the flies are seen no more. Why have you people decided to trail us to our hiding place? Or have you come to also conspire to eject us from here?

FIRST YOUTH: (*prostrates*) great king of Aneile!

ONUCHOWGU: Did I hear you say king of Aneile?

YOUTHS: Your highness; you are still our king.

ONUCHOWGU: (*angrily*) listen; you fool! What a child fears to see in the day time, he does not pray to see at night. The throne of Aneile has led me from grace to grass. I now see it as a nightmare when you address me as your king. Besides, Aneile sons and daughters with the exception of my wife, Enemaku and his family are but emblems of calamity!

SECOND YOUTH: Your highness, we have come in peace.

ONUCHOWGU: Even if you have not come in peace, do you think that bothers me? Or don't you know that the sight of a catapult does not scare an already gunned down bird? Can you do worse than you have done?

AJANIGO: By the way, what are you trio doing here?

ENEMAKU: As if you knew what was in my mind.

YOUTHS: The gods have finally spoken!!

ONUCHOWGU: (*after a pause*) what did they say?

THIRD YOUTH: The chiefs conspired with his in-law in Dekina to get the district head ruled against you and Aduku was bought off on his way from Idah and made to change the verdict of Atta's Court in favour of the Chiefs.

ALL: What!!!

ANIBE: How could Aduku do this to the king?

ONUCHOWGU: Who told you all these?

FIRST YOUTH: My lord, calamity took over Aneile. Strange maladies attacked our people. The people began to die in hundreds. Our crops were drying up and our animals were falling. The only remedy the King could provide for us was to send his killer squad after us to suppress opposition from any quarters. We responded by matching to the palace to attack him. It was while we were at the palace that Atebo, the Chief Priest of the Royal Ancestral Shrine appeared and revealed everything to us.

ONUCHOWGU: You mean the Chief Priest of the Royal Ancestral Shrine came from Idah to reveal this to you?

YOUTHS: Yes your highness.

ONUCHOWGU: By the way, who is your new king?

SECOND YOUTH: Ogecha, the mouthpiece of the gods.

(*Everybody expresses shock and disappointment*)

ONUCHOWGU: (*smile sarcastically*) Ogecha and his cohorts have forgotten that all food can be stolen and consumed without been discovered through the mouth of the thief but not the locust bean. Now they know the gods and the ancestral spirits are much alive to their responsibilities.

AJANIGO: (*bows and worship the gods*) the gods of our ancestors, we worship you. The gods of our forefathers we adore you. You have done this for us? You are indeed worthy to be praised. We say thank you from the bottom of our hearts.

ONUCHOWGU: What then is your mission here?

THIRD YOUTH: The Oracle said that if in seven days we have not brought you back to the throne of Aneile, the world's calamities will converge on Aneile and condemn us to permanent destruction.

FIRST YOUTH: Extinction precisely!

ONUCHOWGU: Youths of Aneile, the spot a child dreads in the day time, he does not go there at night. Aneile is a merciless whipping masquerade that I cannot afford to be chased by. I am not going back there.

AJANIGO: Yes! My lord, we are not going!

YOUTHS: (*kneel*) your highness, please forgive us and return home.

ONUCHOWGU: The day a baby leaves the womb is the day it completes its assignment in the womb. I have no work left undone before my departure from Aneile. So, what am I going there to do?

SECOND YOUTH: Your highness, failure to return to Aneile spells doom for us.

ONUCHOWGU: That is my exact wish! The hen that searches for crumbs beneath hot embers must be prepared to be a cripple. A woman who breastfeeds a viper must be prepared to die of the viper's venom. You have fanned the embers of calamity and you shall be consumed by it!

YOUTHS: Your highness, we are sorry. It was all a mistake.

ONUCHOWGU: (*to Enemaku*) hear them call it a mistake. A mistake! You said you treasure the frog meat in your food that without it you go sorrowing and now you have seen a frog and have foolishly mistaken it to be a toad and have let it go; you would have to endure the sorrow of consuming your soup without the aromatic delicacy of the thighs of the frog.

THIRD YOUTH: Your highness, you elders say that the tooth the leopard uses to chastise its babies is the same tooth it uses in lifting them to safe spots when enemies are sighted. We regret our misdeeds and we are sincerely sorry.

ONUCHOWGU: You show the bitter leaf tree contempt and disregard it because it grows on your sugar cane farm; now that you are sick, the herbalist prepares its juice for your quick recovery and you think the indignant bitter leaf would allow you drink its juice without a commensurate bitter resentment in your mouth. How can that be possible?!

YOUTHS: Your highness, it will never happen again.

FIRST YOUTH: Your highness, all we are asking for is a second chance.

ONUCHOWGU: If you give a second chance to a rampaging elephant to tread on you, you are sure to be bidding farewell to mother-earth. I can't give a second chance to an obvious destruction like Aneile.

SECOND YOUTH: (*cleans his tear-filled eyes*) your highness, have mercy on us and remember the innocent ones among us that did not support the plot.

ONUCHOWGU: The fisherman who listens to the plea of a fish to be allowed to drink its last water from the stream, would either disappoint his waiting customers or would consume his pudding without the aroma of a fish. The only assets I have are my family and my dignity as a human. I will not allow Aneile to trick me to lose them.

YOUTHS: (*tearfully*) please your highness. We beg you. Please and please.

ENEMAKU: (*sympathetically*) my lord, a headache cannot be too severe for a man to cut off his head to gain relief. Aneile has hurt you beyond limit but they have paid the price for their evil and now they are sorry. This is the right time for my lord to demonstrate one of the greatest but most difficult of all virtues on earth – spirit of forgiveness.

ONUCHOWGU: Enemaku, you see; the mother–snake is a wise animal who cautions the mother–hen that no amount of love shown to one's offerings can prevent them from rebelling against one; that is why the snake carries no babies as the hen does; but like the hen I disrespected the wisdom of the snake and turned deaf ears to its warnings. Now events have unfolded themselves; at the end of it all, here I am with painful injuries inflicted on me by the babies I had carried and cherished as my flesh and blood. Don't you now see that it would be sheer stupidity to repeat the mistake that had almost ruined me?

ENEMAKU: Your majesty, please forgive them for the sake of the gods and our ancestors.

YOUTHS: (*soaked in tears*) please your highness, forgive us and spare us from more calamities.

ONUCHOWGU: No matter how charming is the smile on the face of a tiger; the rabbit does not get infatuated by it as to yearn for its companionship. Even your tears cannot move me!

ENEMAKU: My lord, don't forget the gods sent these young men to go and bring you back to the throne of Aneile. If you fail them, the gods and the ancestral spirits may turn their backs on you.

AJANIGO: (*nods in support*) my lord, I agree with Elder Enemaku. No one disobeys the call of the gods. You have to reconsider your stance. The call is a sign of honour and love from the gods, your rejection may be met with disgrace and chastisement.

ONUCHOWGU: (*after a pause*) both of you are correct. My only fear is the perception I have of the throne of Aneile.

ENEMAKU: What perception your majesty?

ONUCHOWGU: I see the throne of Aneile as a royal mat but a spider's web in disguise; sitting on it may mean having excruciating swollen buttocks from regular fall. I now dread their throne.

ENEMAKU: My lord, the thunder does not strike twice on the same spot. Besides, the one that places the crown of honour on you shall always protect it from falling down. Moreover, you don't fear for the divinity what humanity cannot control. Let the gods' responsibilities be left for them to ponder over or worry about.

EJURA: That is true your majesty, whether or not you are a king, a destined misfortune shall always find a way to mark its presence in the life of its destined host. The most interesting thing is that the affliction of a good man would always receive the attention of the good gods.

ANIBE: Your highness, the revelation and the call have shown that the gods and the ancestral spirits are on your side.

OKPANANCHI: Father; it will be daring to reject their calls.

ATULUKU: Father; we have to honour their calls and to go back to Aneile.

ENEMAKU: My lord, if a sick man considers the bitterness of herbs, he will never consume them and be cured; what he considers is the restoration of health the consumption of the herbs brings to him. You have to return to Aneile because of the gods and not because of Aneile people.

ONUCHOWGU: (*convinced; solus*) hun! A bitter herb is not consumed because of the love for bitter herbs but for the curative effect of its juice. In other words, if you cannot consume a roasted yam because of palm oil, you have to consume the palm oil because of the roasted yam. The gods and not the people should be the reason behind my decision to return to Aneile. (*To the crowd*) Is that not what you are all saying?

ALL: Yes your highness.

ONUCHOWGU: (*heave a sigh of relief*) I give up. I believe all of you and I totally agree with what you have said. In addition to that, I have also realized that today one may be on the wronged and forgiving side, tomorrow he may find himself on the erring and apologizing side; and let it be known that for those we have wronged to forgive us, we must learn to forgive those who have wronged us. Youths of Aneile, stand up; I have forgiven Aneile.

YOUTHS: (*excitedly*) thank you my lord.

ONUCHOWGU: (*stands up*) my people, after the day's work, where does a farmer go to?

ALL: (*excitedly*) home!!!

ONUCHOWGU: Then stand up, arrange our luggage and let us go back to where we belong!

There is great excitement among them as everybody except the youths exchange warm embraces with the king and then hurries out of the stage. Lights fade out.

ACT SEVEN SCENE FOUR

Ebiloma and Ocheja sit facing Abalaka and Idachaba with heads down and engrossed in deep meditation. Silence engulfs the stage. Enter Omale looking moody.

OMALE: Chiefs of Aneile, Aduku is dead! (*The chiefs are not shocked by the news*) I said Aduku is dead! (*No response*) am I talking to logs of woods? Aduku is dead I said!!

EBILOMA: And then! Do you want us to behead ourselves because Aduku is dead?!

OMALE: (*surprised; after a pause*) I mean the poor boy you threatened his life to change the verdict of Atta's court is dead and you are asking me whether you should behead yourselves!

OCHEJA: What do you expect us to do or say about it?

OMALE: Can't you at least mourn him for a little while?

IDACHABA: Elder Omale, of what use are the tears of a dying man for a dead man when both of them are heading to the same destination and only been separated by a twinkle of an eye distance? Have you not realized that the same fate awaits us?!

ABALAKA: Besides, no one expects a message of condolence from anyone when everyone is bereaved. Or tell us who among us has not suffered one misfortune or the other. My family cannot even count its loss. Ebiloma lost his two daughters. Ocheja lost his twins. Idachaba lost his three sons and Ogecha's children are all lying critically ill with no hope of recovery. Even you; have you finished mourning the death of your only son?

OMALE: (*gives in; sits*) you are right. It is very unfortunate.

Ogecha enters

OGECHA: Chiefs look at what you have done to me?!

EBILOMA: Wise one, what have we done to you?

OGECHA: I am on the verge of losing my entire family to incurable maladies.

OCHEJA: How is that our making?

OGECHA: If you had not involved me in your evil plot, none of these calamities would have befallen me!

IDACHABA: But you enjoyed it while it lasted!

ABALAKA: After all, you wore the crown, sat on Aneile throne and enjoyed all privileges and honour of a king. What greatness on earth is more than that?

OGECHA: What greatness?! Don't you know that a beggar on the street is better than a disfavored and disgraced king? Of what honour is the mane to a lion been consumed by fire? I am doomed; can't you get it?!

OCHEJA: Wise one, whose roof does the heavy downpour doesn't wet? Have you forgotten that the sprinkled devil bean powder does not know whose skin is of a royal blood? We are all doomed!

EBILOMA: Besides, the finger tip of the child has already been cut off; whether it was the knife that was wicked or it was the child that was reckless is a matter of no importance as what has happened has happened; the finger tip is off!

(*Omale shakes his head expressing sorrow*)

IDACHABA: (*after a pause*) It was our entire fault. We were hunters; we saw and mistook the tigers for mere fat cats and we hunted them with mere rods; now we have become the hunted; the aggrieved tigers are now rampaging with deadly teeth and claws. What do we do?!

OGECHA: There is nothing we can do about it. The goat that chooses the den of hyenas as its grazing field cannot be saved even by magic.

OMALE: But this is too much!

OCHEJA: What do you expect?! He, who gets infatuated by the delicacy of a pudding prepared in a large pot and chooses to satisfy the infatuation by consuming without end, must be prepared to suffer the pains of incurable constipation.

ABALAKA: We were too audacious!

EBILOMA: Sometimes it is good to be audacious but I think we have allowed our audacity to grow into madness by chasing after a fish in a river overpopulated by sharks. We have fought the anointed of the gods and the gods are now on the loose!

OGECHA: We did more than that; we also wrestled with the gods by daring to alter the course of destiny of another man and using deceit, falsehood and oppression to bring calamity to innocent people. I tried my best to appease them to forgive us but they refused. In fact I can't even go near the shrine anymore since the day Atebo visited the shrine and performed certain sacrifices to the gods.

OMALE: My worry is that if the mother-hen slumps and dies; what befalls the newly hatched chicks in the mist of the enemies that killed their mother? What would happen to our wives and children after we die?

IDACHABA: That is if they don't all die before us.

EBILOMA: (*after a pause*) wise one, elder Omale, my fellow chiefs, I think we should not totally condemn ourselves. Every step we take in life is a risk no matter our intentions. If a man is lucky, his steps take him to glory but if he is unlucky, his steps bring him to ruin. If we end our lives in an unpleasant manner, it is not because we have chosen it for ourselves; it is the maker of our destinies that have been unfair to us for we all are actors; the earth is our stage; destiny is the script; the Supreme Being is the writer. We can only act the contents of the scripts as written in our destinies. If every man had been given the opportunity to choose; a king might choose to be a slave in his world and a slave a king. On our part, we were destined to tread on the wrong path of evil; we have trodden it so well that we have now gotten to the point of no return. We have been condemned to be inflicted by strange illnesses and be thrown to the evil forest and then die! (*Stands up*) But before such a thing happens to me, I have resolved to take my own life! An overripe fruit submits itself in peace to the mother-earth rather than wait for aggressive stones of passers-by to knock it down (*tearfully*) .It is sad for me to bid farewell to all of you. Let me make it clear to you that if I happen to come back to mother-earth again, you would always be my chosen companions and associates. It is time to part ways; if destiny wishes, we shall meet again may be to part no more but if it doesn't, then so be it; it was beautiful working with you. My people, goodbye to you all! (*Exit*)

ALL: (*shocked; stand up*) Ebiloma!! Ebiloma!! Ebiloma!!

(*Everybody wails mourning the departure of Ebiloma*)

OCHEJA: (*stands up furiously*) Ebiloma has taken the right step. Shame is a calamity that is worse than death. I have also made up my mind to end my life in the same manner. Therefore it is time to say goodbye to you all. (*Exit*)

ALL: Ocheja!! Ocheja!! Ocheja!!

IDACHABA: (*stands up hesitantly*) A journey is finished when a destination is sighted. I have seen my final above beyond and there I go now! Adieu my people. (*Exit*)

ALL: Idachaba!! Idachaba!! Idachaba!!

ABALAKA: (*On his feet*) everything has an end; so is every man. My people, I pray we meet again. (*Exit*)

OGECHA & OMALE: Abalaka!! Abalaka!! Abalaka!!

OMALE: (*Walks away slowly and turns back to face Ogecha*) If the foundation of a house goes down, the house does not stand. I have also sighted my destination; and so my journey has ended. Wise one, this is the right time to say goodbye. (*Exit*)

OGECHA: Omale! Omale!! Omale!!! (*After a pause*) What am I waiting for? Where a child dares to play, an old man does not dread it. Besides, I can't watch myself being taken to the evil forest alive under the humiliation of a strange and incurable illness. (*After a pause*) my desire, my desire, my desire; see where you have landed me. Had I know that the death of every man lies in his own desire, I would not have desired when desires were not desirable. But here I am an apostle of bad desires and a victim of their deadly consequences. Well, I guess it was meant to be. (*Exit*)

There is a dirge. Lights fade out.

ACT SEVEN SCENE FIVE

There is drumming, singing and dancing in the palace.

SOLO: whe f'ewo wa o (2x) – come to our land

CHORUS: Onuchowgu whe f'ewo wa – come to our land Onuchowgu

SOLO: Onu weche o whe che o – you are king; come to our land

CHORUS: Repeat chorus

SOLO: Ene lile o whe f'ewo wa – great man, please come to our land

CHORUS: Repeat chorus

SOLO: Naa wu yin whe o ke wa chonu – Come to your land and be a king

CHORUS: idu idu o idu idu onu weche o idu idu – lion, lion, you are a king, lion, lion.

(Enter Onuchowgu accompanied by his family. Three old women

make a traditional hooting to which the town's people respond will joyful yell. They all pay homage. Onuchowgu sits and his family members also make themselves comfortable)

ANIBE: Aneile people, the king greets you.

TOWN'S PEOPLE: Onu jaaashi!!!

ONE CITIZEN: Your highness, we thank you for your forgiveness in spite of all our atrocities. We have all resolved never to allow such a thing happen again. Whenever we are given raw tubers of yam to consume, we will always remember when we ate raw yam and suffer severe itching in our mouths. Once again we are sorry your highness.

(A young man rushes in panting and pays homage)

ONUCHOWGU: Young man, what is the matter?

THE YOUNG MAN: *(gasping for breath)* your highness..........
the mouth…...pie…ce of the gods, elder Ogecha……..and … and…Chiefs Ebiloma, Ocheja, Idachaba, Abalaka and elder Omale…….*(stops and pants)*

ONUCHOWGU: *(curious)* ehen, what happened to them?!

THE YOUNG MAN: My lord, they are dead!

(Town's people express shock)

ONUCHOWGU: Where, how and when?!

THE YOUNG MAN: They committed suicide in their respective houses!

ONUCHOWGU: *(rhetorically)* suicide?!

(Atebo enters and pay homage)

ATEBO: Your highness, don't be surprised. Men who wrestle

150

with their gods are like trees that wrestle with their soils; they will come to ruin! The eggs that lock horns with stones would waste! Greed wastes a man faster than a bullet wastes a maggot. When a man allows greed to get hold of him, he begins to desire to unseat his own maker; his desires go on and on until they turn him to a drunken antelope that remains adamant to graze in the den of the most dangerous army of lions; such a man like such an antelope would face a calamity in its most cruel form! Those men have by their own hands dug their own graves and we must quickly help in burying them with all pleasure. Their corpses must not see the next dawn in Aneile. Whatever declares itself as excrement is not meant for one's pot of soup; it is meant for the bush. Their bodies must be dumped in the evil forest to rot. This is a lesson for all of you who may be treading the same evil path as they have trodden to be careful about what you desire and to know that every evil you do against a fellow man would someday come back to hunt and kill you. Let it be also known to you that every man's destiny is the work of his maker; if you try to push a man against the order of his destiny, you wrestle with the man's maker and the consequences are calamitous. As for you Onuchowgu, the gods and the ancestral spirits welcome you back to Aneile.

ONUCHOWGU: Thank you the Custodian of the Royal Ancestral Shrine. I appreciate your quick intervention into the calamity that befell Aneile.

ATEBO: I only did what the gods sent me.

ONUCHOWGU: Your promptness in doing it is highly appreciated.

ATEBO: Your highness, thank you for the compliments.

ONUCHOWGU: Wise one, the pleasure is mine.

ATEBO: Your highness, it is time for you to know something that would interest you.

ONUCHOWGU: (*curiously*) what is it wise one?

ATEBO: Be patient; I will tell you everything. (*After a pause*) Your late father Ilemona knew himself as a slave but he wasn't. He was a true son of Aneile.

(*Everybody expresses shock*)

ONUCHOWGU: (*awe-struck*) what! Wise one, is it a joke or what?

ATEBO: (*jokingly*) do I look like a clown, your highness?

ONUCHOWGU: (Curiously) please wise one, I am all ears.

ATEBO: This is how it happened:

There is a FLASH BACK as light fades out on the palace and shines on an ancient hut. Two men are seated as the third man identified as Opaluwa enters and sits.

OPALUWA: Chiefs of Aneile, you are welcome.

CHIEFS: Thank you elder Opaluwa.

OPALUWA: I have called all of you here for an urgent matter.

CHIEFS: We are all ears.

OPALUWA: You know that since the death of Ukwenya our late king, Ilemona his only heir to the throne has been ill and have failed to recover in spite the efforts of our best herbalists.

CHIEFS: What do you suggest we do?

OPALUWA: Good question! That is why I have called you both here. Since I am the only surviving brother of the late king, why don't I take over the throne?

FIRST CHIEF: What then happens to Ilemona?

OPALUWA: Another good question! I am thinking of sending him into slavery to a distant land possibly to Nupe land.

SECOND CHIEF: What will you tell the town's people?

OPALUWA: Good question once more! I intend to tell them that a foreign herbalist has been invited and he has found that he suffers a demonic attack that would require spiritual cleansing over a long period of time and would have to be taken far away from Aneile to avoid been seen by anyone throughout the duration of the cleansing.

FIRST CHIEF: That's a clever arrangement.

SECOND CHIEF: Elder Opaluwa, what do we stand to gain from supporting your plot?

OPALUWA: Excellent question! An obedient dog does not go hungry when its master's success in hunting is to its credit. I shall make you richer and greater than you can ever imagine. Just wait and let me get to the throne first.

CHIEFS: Then you have our absolute support!!

(Lights fade out and shine on Atebo)

That was how Ilemona your late father was sold into slavery to Nupe land under the disguise of spiritual cleansing. But the gods were in control of the situation. Ilemona later recovered and escaped. After so many days of travelling he met a native doctor from Abejukolo who was hunting for herbs and spiritual materials in the heart of the forest closed to Nupe land. The native doctor took him to his house where he lived as his apprentice until his demise. Shortly after then, he took up hunting as a profession and one day found himself in the forest of Aneile and arrested by the village guards having been labeled a spy. All these were the designs of the gods to bring him back to the throne of his father. The rest of the story is known to you all.

TOWN'S PEOPLE: (*in awe*) hee eee eeeeeeeh!!!!!!

ONUCHOWGU: (*Dumb founded; grab his head with his hands*) wise one, this is unbelievable!

ATEBO: Your highness, it is indeed incredible but that was what your late father went through.

ONUCHOWGU: But wise one, how come my father forgot his origin?

ATEBO: Opaluwa his uncle fed him with certain concussions that made him forget everything about his own past. The only thing he knew and remembered was his slavery status and that was the only thing he could tell you.

ONUCHOWGU: Wise one, how did you know this story since you were not physically present?

ATEBO: Your highness, where on earth do the eyes of the gods not see?

ONUCHOWGU: (*struggles to find tears*) Oh my poor father! Why did the gods not reveal this evil to Aneile People and allowed it to get this far? Why were they silent for so long?

ATEBO: Your highness, the ways of the gods are not the ways of man. They are mysterious in their doings. No one questions their decisions. If the gods are to react the way we mortals react, this earth would surely not have survived this long. The most interesting thing is that their chosen times are always the best. Your father's case is a living testimony to that. The gods caused a mysterious fire to consume Opaluwa and his cohorts and then hardened the heart of King Abutu to engage Aneile in battle with the aim of using your father to rescue Aneile thereby paving way for him to ascend his throne. And here you are, continuing from where he stopped. Are they not worthy of adoration?

ONUCHOWGU: (*pleased*) they are indeed worthy of all adoration and worship.

ATEBO: Your highness; who and where is your closest friend?

ONUCHOWGU: (*calling*) Enemaku!

ENEMAKU: (*comes forward*) your highness!

ONUCHOWGU: (*points at him*) wise one, here he is.

ATEBO: He has been chosen by the gods as your new Chief Priest!

ENEMAKU: (*surprised*) I, a Chief Priest?!

ATEBO: So declared the gods. I will come back by the next Aneile market day to give you the tips that you would need to effectively discharge your sacred duties.

ENEMAKU: (*still surprised*) thank you wise one.

ATEBO: All thanks are to the gods.

ONUCHOWGU: Wise one we shall be expecting you.

ATEBO: Lest I forget; your highness, your people must make some sacrifices to appease the gods and cleanse the land for joining in revolting not just against you but against the gods. The sacrificial items include seven white he-goats, seven white cocks, twenty one native cola nuts, seven yards of white cloth, seven gourds of palm wine, seven gourds of palm oil and seven baskets of fried been cake. All shall be brought to the village ancestral shrine on your next market day. I shall be there to assist Enemaku to perform the sacrifices. (*After a pause*) It is time for me to go.

ONUCHOWGU: Wise one, on behalf of Aneile people, I say thank you and farewell. May the gods and the ancestral spirits go with you.

ATEBO: Thank you, your highness.(*Exit; amidst admiration by the town's people*)

ONUCHOWGU: My people; let us go home. Tomorrow is a day for a greater celebration. Let the masqueraders prepare our great masquerades – *Olageyin, Egu Opia, Egu Babi, Egu Ebo, Egu Gbomgbom, Egu Afia, Ukpoku* and *Egu Ogba* and let us meet at the village square tomorrow. All the village drummers and dancers are also expected to be present……... My people, when the stomach is relieved of pains, the heart jubilates! When a partridge is to be shot and the hunter's bullet finishes, the partridge jumps up in intense delight! When an egg thrown out lands on soft sands, mother hen celebrates! Celebrate my people!

Town's people yell in ecstasy; sing and dance. Onuchowgu and his family are seen hugging one another. Light fades out.

-----THE END------

EPILOGUE

Light shines on the center stage. The NARRATOR appears.

NARRATOR:

There is always a day of reckoning for everything we do on earth. Contentment is a virtue man must strive for; with it, greed runs from the heart of man but without it greed ruins the soul of man. Whatever is not destined to be yours will never be yours'. If you seize it by force, you will relinquish it by force; If not by the force of man, surely by the force of the Supreme Being. Let justice, love and peace be the rulers of your hearts. Watch your steps and be careful of the path you tread; for our steps and our paths in life would always determine our fates and destinations both here and in hereafter.

Leaders who abuse their powers, rulers who are indifferent to the plights of their people and are intolerant of opposition, the rich who oppress the poor, strong men who oppress the weak, people who plot the down fall of innocent men, those who kill their fellow men unjustly, those who plot to alter the destiny of another man, those who challenge the will of GOD, those who derive pleasure

157

in iniquities, evils and atrocities, those who tell lies in the name of GOD, those who use obscene and profane words against GOD, those who do not believe that there is GOD and those who worship gods other than GOD are THE MEN WHO WRESTLE WITH GOD and like Ogecha, Ebiloma, Ocheja, Abalaka, Idachaba, Omale and their cohorts, they will surely come to ruin.